TAIPE GUIDE 2024

The Ultimate Guide to Taiwan's Lively Urban Hub - Taipei!

Leo Merritt

3

Welcome to Taipei

Welcome to Taipei, a captivating metropolis nestled between the emerald mountains and the sparkling blue waters of northern Taiwan. In this vibrant city, ancient traditions harmoniously coexist with cutting-edge modernity, creating an unparalleled tapestry of culture, cuisine, and charm.

Taipei is cradled within a lush basin, bordered by the majestic Yangmingshan National Park to the north and the soothing Danshui River to the west. The city's geography lends itself to stunning vistas, offering panoramic views of Taipei 101, the iconic skyscraper that pierces the sky like a bamboo shoot.

Beyond the city's limits, verdant mountains and serene hot springs await, inviting you to immerse yourself in nature's embrace. Taipei is a thriving business hub, teeming with bustling streets and vibrant markets. The city's economy is fueled by its industries in technology, electronics, and finance, making it a hotbed of innovation and entrepreneurship.

Amidst the hustle and bustle, you'll find modern office buildings housing dynamic professionals from around the world, adding to the city's cosmopolitan allure. Taipei's rich history and diverse heritage are evident in its architecture, art, and cuisine.

From the graceful Longshan Temple to the contemporary exhibits at Huashan 1914 Creative Park, the city embraces its past while embracing innovation. In the heart of it all, the Raohe Street Night Market and Shilin Night Market offer a tantalizing journey through Taiwan's culinary delights, showcasing the essence of Taipei's cultural melting pot.

The way of life in Taipei is a delicate balance of tradition and modern living. The city's inhabitants, known for their hospitality, embrace both their roots and the excitement of urban living. You'll witness locals gathering at traditional tea houses for leisurely chats, while others indulge in the vibrant nightlife that light up the city's streets after dark.

Throughout the year, Taipei comes alive with lively festivals and celebrations, each offering a glimpse into the city's cultural soul. The Lunar New Year welcomes the Year of the Pig with dazzling dragon dances, while the mesmerizing Lantern Festival illuminates the night sky with a sea of colorful lanterns.

These events provide an opportunity to immerse yourself in the vibrant traditions and warm camaraderie of Taipei's locals. Navigating Taipei is a breeze, thanks to its efficient public transportation system. The Taipei Metro (MRT) connects key neighborhoods and attractions, while buses offer extensive coverage throughout the city. Bike-sharing programs pedestrian-friendly streets make exploring Taipei on foot or by bicycle a delightful option.

Taipei's futuristic spirit is evident in its embrace of technology. As a global leader in innovation, the city boasts high-speed internet, smart infrastructure, and a seamless digital experience that enhances everyday life. At the heart of Taipei lies its most precious gem - the warmth of Taiwanese hospitality.

The locals' genuine smiles and open-hearted nature welcome visitors with open arms, making you feel at home in this bustling urban wonderland. With its captivating landscapes, vibrant culture, and dynamic way of life, Taipei invites you to immerse yourself in a city where every moment is an adventure waiting to unfold.

Are you seeking the tranquility of nature or the excitement of urban exploration? Taipei offers a tapestry of experiences that will forever leave an indelible mark on your heart. Welcome to Taipei - a city that captures the essence of Taiwan's past, present, and future in a captivating embrace. Let your journey of discovery begin!

Why Choose Taipei for Your Adventure

Welcome to the enchanting world of Taipei, where East meets West, tradition dances with modernity, and every street corner tells a story waiting to be discovered. As an insider, I invite you to embark on an adventure like no other—a journey that will leave you mesmerized, enriched, and forever captivated by the city's charm.

A Tapestry of Cultures:

As you step into the heart of Taipei, you'll find a city that beautifully weaves together a tapestry of cultures. In the historic streets of Dadaocheng, the scent of freshly brewed tea drifts through the air, hinting at Taiwan's rich tea-drinking heritage. Meanwhile, in the vibrant Ximending district, neon lights illuminate the bustling streets, showcasing the city's dynamic youth culture. Taipei's seamless blend of tradition and modernity creates an exhilarating backdrop for your adventure.

Culinary Wonderland:

Prepare to indulge your taste buds in a culinary wonderland. Taipei's night markets are a haven for foodies, offering an array of delectable treats that will ignite your senses. Sink your teeth into piping hot stinky tofu, savor the sweet melody of bubble tea, and feast on mouthwatering dumplings. Each bite is an invitation to explore the city's diverse flavors and savor its culinary soul.

Nature's Oasis:

Beyond the city's bustling streets, nature beckons you to explore its scenic wonders. A short journey to Yangmingshan National Park reveals a breathtaking landscape of rolling hills, hot springs, and colorful flower fields. As you hike the trails, the crisp mountain air embraces you like an old friend, offering a moment of tranquility amidst the urban buzz.

Temples of Serenity:

In Taipei, spirituality finds expression in its majestic temples. The Longshan Temple stands as a symbol of resilience, having weathered centuries of history and still captivating visitors with its intricate architecture. The air is thick with the fragrance of incense, and the soft glow of lanterns casts a magical aura, inviting you to immerse yourself in the city's spiritual heritage.

Embrace Local Traditions:

Taipei invites you to participate in its vibrant traditions. As you stroll through the streets during the Lunar New Year, the city comes alive with dragon dances and lantern festivals. Experience the grace of a traditional tea ceremony, where the art of tea-making is steeped in respect and harmony. By embracing these customs, you become part of Taipei's living tapestry of traditions.

Warmth of Taiwanese Hospitality:

Beyond Taipei's architectural wonders and culinary delights, it is the warmth of Taiwanese hospitality that leaves a lasting impression. The locals' genuine smiles and willingness to share their culture make you feel like a welcomed guest rather than a tourist. Their warmth and friendliness create a sense of belonging, turning your adventure into an unforgettable journey of connections.

Modern Marvels:

Taipei's forward-thinking spirit is evident in its modern marvels. Gaze in awe at the iconic Taipei 101, a feat of engineering that pierces the sky like a bamboo shoot. The city's efficient public transportation system, high-speed trains, and modern infrastructure exemplify a city that embraces progress while preserving its heritage.

Art and Creativity:

As you explore Taipei's creative hubs, you'll discover a vibrant art scene that celebrates diversity and imagination. Visit the Huashan 1914 Creative Park, where the old warehouse complex has been transformed into a hub of artistic expression. Engage with local artists, immerse yourself in thought-provoking exhibits, and let the city's creativity inspire your own sense of wonder.

Safe and Welcoming:

Taipei is not just an adventure; it's a safe haven for travelers. The city's low crime rate and friendly atmosphere make it a welcoming destination for solo explorers and families alike. The sense of security allows you to venture into hidden alleys and embrace the city's nooks and crannies without hesitation.

A Symphony of Lights:

As day turns to night, Taipei transforms into a mesmerizing symphony of lights. The city's skyline is adorned with a kaleidoscope of colors, and the iconic Rainbow Bridge dances with shimmering reflections on the water. The vibrant nightlife beckons you to embrace the energy of the city, igniting a sense of wonder as you discover the magic of Taipei after dark.

So, dear adventurer, why choose Taipei for your journey? It's a city that will ignite your senses, captivate your heart, and welcome you with open arms. Taipei is more than a destination; it's an experience that will leave you forever enchanted, beckoning you to return and rediscover its magic time and time again. Come, embrace the adventure, and let Taipei unveil its secrets to you like an old friend sharing cherished stories. Your adventure awaits!

Before You Go

Best Time to Visit Taipei

Hey there, fellow traveler! I'm excited to help you find the best time to visit Taipei. As an insider, I'll let you in on the secrets of this incredible city's seasonal charm. So, whether you're planning a cultural exploration, a food adventure, or an outdoor escapade, let's dive into the details together!

Spring - A Tapestry of Blossoms:

Ah, springtime in Taipei is truly magical! From late February to early April, the city transforms into a mesmerizing tapestry of cherry blossoms and azaleas. Head to Yangmingshan National Park or Taipei Expo Park witness nature's dazzling show of colors. It's the perfect time to immerse yourself in the beauty of blooming flora.

Summer - Embrace the Festive Spirit:

Welcome to Taipei's vibrant summer! From June to August, the city comes alive with festive events and cultural celebrations. Don't miss the Dragon Boat Festival, where you can witness exhilarating boat races along the Keelung River. The spirited atmosphere and warm weather make it ideal for night market adventures and indulging in refreshing summer treats.

Autumn - A Symphony of Colors:

Taipei's autumn is an artist's palette of golden hues. From September to November, the city's parks and mountains are dressed in stunning fall foliage. Yangmingshan and Jiufen offer picturesque landscapes that will leave you breathless. It's a time to savor the crisp air, enjoy outdoor hikes, and capture postcard-perfect moments.

Winter - Cozy Comforts and Hot Springs:

Winter in Taipei offers a different kind of charm. From December to February, the temperatures dip, creating a cozy ambiance. It's the perfect time to indulge in hot pot dinners and traditional Taiwanese stews. Don't forget to warm up in one of Beitou's natural hot springs for an ultimate relaxation experience.

Year-Round Attractions:

While each season has its unique charm, some attractions in Taipei remain open and captivating all year long. For example, the National Palace Museum houses a treasure trove of Chinese artifacts regardless of the season. Likewise, Taipei 101's observation deck provides breathtaking city views all year round.

Consideration for Crowds:

Keep in mind that Taipei experiences a surge in tourism during peak seasons, especially during Chinese New Year (January or February). If you prefer fewer crowds and more affordable rates, consider visiting during shoulder seasons like early spring or late autumn.

Weather-Appropriate Attire:

Taipei's weather varies from season to season, so it's essential to pack weather-appropriate attire. Light and breathable clothing for summer, layers for spring and autumn, and warm clothing for winter will ensure you're comfortable throughout your trip.

Conclusion:

There you have it—the best time to visit Taipei, each season offering its own captivating allure. Whether you're drawn to the blooming flowers of spring, the vibrant festivities of summer, the colorful foliage of autumn, or the cozy comforts of winter, Taipei awaits your discovery. Plan your visit according to your preferences, and get ready for an extraordinary adventure in this lively city. Happy travels!

Visa and Entry Requirements

Fellow adventurer! Let's dive into the essential topic of visa and entry requirements for visiting Taipei. As an insider, I'm here to guide you through the process and help you plan a smooth and hassle-free entry into this vibrant city. Let's get started!

Visa Exemption and Visa on Arrival:

Great news! Taipei offers visa exemptions and visa on arrival for citizens of many countries. For short visits, travelers from eligible countries can enter Taiwan without applying for a visa in advance. The duration of the visa-free stay varies depending on your nationality, so make sure to check the specific requirements for your country.

Visitor Visa Application:

If your country is not eligible for visa exemption or visa on arrival, don't worry! Applying for a visitor visa is straightforward. You'll need to contact the nearest Taiwan embassy or consulate in your home country to obtain the necessary application forms and guidelines.

Required Documents:

When applying for a visitor visa, you'll typically need to provide a few essential documents. These may include a valid passport with at least six months validity, a completed visa application form, passport-sized photos, flight itinerary, hotel reservation, and proof of sufficient funds to cover your stay in Taipei.

Invitation Letters and Supporting Documents:

If you're visiting Taipei for specific purposes, such as business meetings, conferences, or academic activities, you might need additional documents. An invitation letter from your host in Taipei, along with supporting documents explaining the purpose of your visit, can be valuable in the visa application process.

Processing Time and Fees:

Visa processing times can vary, depending on the embassy or consulate and the type of visa you're applying for. It's advisable to apply well in advance of your travel dates to avoid any last-minute delays. Keep in mind that there is usually a visa application fee, which also varies based on your nationality and visa type.

Entry Stamps and Arrival Procedures:

Once you arrive in Taipei, you'll be issued an entry stamp at the immigration checkpoint. This stamp will indicate the duration of your permitted stay in Taiwan. It's crucial to be aware of the allowed stay period to avoid any overstay issues, as overstaying can result in fines or other penalties.

Extensions and Overstays:

If you wish to extend your stay beyond the permitted period, you can apply for an extension at the National Immigration Agency in Taiwan. However, keep in mind that overstaying without proper permission is taken seriously, and it's best to adhere to the entry requirements and visa regulations.

Conclusion:

There you have it—a detailed overview of visa and entry requirements for your Taipei adventure! Whether you're eligible for visa exemption, applying for a visitor visa, or planning to extend your stay, understanding the entry procedures is essential. Always check with the official Taiwanese authorities or consult your nearest embassy or consulate for the most up-to-date and accurate information. Safe travels, and I can't wait to welcome you to this vibrant city!

Currency and Money Matters

Let's delve into the topic of currency and money matters in Taipei. As an insider, I'll walk you through everything you need to know about the local currency, where to exchange money, and how to handle your finances like a pro during your stay. Let's get started!

Currency in Taipei:

The official currency of Taipei and Taiwan is the New Taiwan Dollar (TWD), often abbreviated as NT$ or NTD. It's important to familiarize yourself with the currency denominations, which include coins (NT$1, NT$5, NT$10, NT$50) and banknotes (NT$100, NT$500, NT$1,000).

Exchange Rates and Money Conversion:

Before arriving in Taipei, it's a good idea to check the current exchange rates to get an idea of how much your home currency is worth in New Taiwan Dollars. You can do this online or through currency exchange apps. Keep in mind that exchange rates can fluctuate, so it's best to check them periodically.

Currency Exchange Options:

In Taipei, you'll find various places to exchange your money into New Taiwan Dollars. Airports, major train stations, and banks usually have currency exchange counters. Additionally, some hotels may offer this service, although the rates might not be as favorable. It's a good practice to compare rates and fees before making any exchange.

ATMs and Withdrawals:

ATMs are widely available throughout Taipei, and many of them accept foreign debit and credit cards. Look for ATMs labeled with international card symbols such as PLUS or Cirrus. While withdrawing money from ATMs is convenient, do keep in mind that your home bank might charge you a fee for international transactions, so it's best to check with your bank beforehand.

Credit Card Usage:

Taipei is a modern city, and credit cards are widely accepted at most establishments, especially in tourist areas, hotels, and restaurants. However, it's always good to carry some cash, as smaller vendors, local markets, and street food stalls might prefer cash payments.

Tipping Culture:

In Taipei, tipping is not a common practice. Most hotels and restaurants include a service charge in the bill. However, if you receive exceptional service or want to show appreciation, a small tip will be well-received.

Budgeting for Your Trip:

Planning your budget for Taipei depends on your travel style and preferences. Generally, Taipei offers a wide range of options for all budgets. To get an estimate, consider the cost of accommodation, meals, transportation, attractions, and any additional activities you plan to indulge in.

Conclusion:

There you have it—everything you need to know about currency and money matters in Taipei! Understanding the local currency, exchange options, and budgeting will help you manage your finances with ease during your stay. Whether you choose to exchange cash or use ATMs, Taipei offers a smooth and convenient experience for handling your money. Enjoy your time in this vibrant city, and may your trip be filled with incredible memories!

Language and Communication

Hello, dear traveler! Let's dive into the topic of language and communication in Taipei. As an insider, I'm thrilled to help you navigate through the linguistic landscape and make your interactions in this vibrant city seamless and enjoyable. Let's get started on our language adventure!

Official Languages: The official language of Taiwan is Mandarin Chinese. You'll find that most signs, public announcements, and official documents are in Mandarin. However, don't worry if you don't speak Mandarin fluently; English is widely understood, especially in tourist areas and establishments.

Common Phrases to Get Started:

It's always fun and courteous to learn a few basic phrases in the local language. In Mandarin, saying "hello" is "nǐ hǎo," "thank you" is "xièxiè," and "excuse me" is "bù hǎo yìsi." Simple greetings can go a long way in creating a friendly atmosphere.

Taiwanese Hokkien:

Besides Mandarin, Taiwanese Hokkien is also spoken in Taipei. It's a local dialect, and some older residents may primarily use it in their daily conversations. While not essential, learning a few

Hokkien phrases can be a delightful way to connect with locals and show appreciation for their culture.

English Language Support:

Taipei is a modern and cosmopolitan city, and you'll find English language support in many places. Most hotels, tourist attractions, and restaurants in popular areas have English-speaking staff who can assist you. Additionally, road signs and public transportation announcements often have English translations.

Translation Apps and Tools:

For more complex interactions or if you want to venture off the beaten path, translation apps can be valuable allies. There are various translation apps available that can help you communicate with locals, read menus, and understand signages in real-time.

Non-Verbal Communication:

Remember, language is not just about words; non-verbal communication plays a significant role in connecting with people. A warm smile, nod, or gesture of appreciation can transcend language barriers and create positive interactions.

Cultural Sensitivity:

Embracing the local culture and customs can enhance your communication experiences. For example, addressing people with polite titles like "mister" or "miss" (xiānsheng and xiǎojiě in Mandarin) shows respect in formal settings. Additionally, learning about local customs can help you avoid unintentional misunderstandings.

Patience and Kindness:

Lastly, remember that language barriers may sometimes lead to misunderstandings, but staying patient and kind will always help bridge the gaps. Many locals appreciate your efforts to communicate, even if it's not perfect, and they'll be more than willing to assist you.

Conclusion:

There you have it—insights into language and communication in Taipei! Embrace the opportunity to learn a few phrases, leverage English language support, and be open to non-verbal connections. Communication is not just about words but about understanding and respect. Enjoy your time in Taipei, immerse yourself in the local culture, and let the magic of communication create unforgettable memories!

Exploring the Neighborhoods

Ximending

I'm thrilled to share my personal experience as a first-time explorer of Ximending, Taipei's lively and vibrant district. Get ready to embark on an unforgettable journey with me through the bustling streets, trendy shops, and delicious street food that make Ximending a must-visit destination. Let's dive right in!

Arriving in Ximending:

As I stepped out of the MRT station and into Ximending, the energy of the district immediately engulfed me. The vibrant atmosphere, filled with colorful billboards and lively crowds, was a sight to behold. I felt an instant connection to this urban playground, which is often referred to as Taipei's version of Shibuya in Tokyo.

Exploring the Streets:

Ximending's pedestrian-friendly streets are a treasure trove of experiences. I strolled along the iconic Ximending Red House, a historic landmark turned into a cultural and creative center. The streets were lined with trendy boutiques, quirky shops, and an array of street vendors offering a variety of goods, from fashion accessories to local crafts.

Tasting Local Delights:

The aroma of street food was irresistible, and I couldn't resist sampling some of the local delicacies. From piping hot stinky tofu to crispy chicken cutlet and mouthwatering bubble tea, Ximending's food scene had my taste buds dancing with joy. Each bite was an explosion of flavors that left me craving for more.

Embracing the Nightlife:

As the sun set, Ximending's nightlife came alive. The district transformed into a hub of entertainment and excitement. Street performers showcased their talents, drawing crowds with mesmerizing acts. The energy was infectious, and I found myself cheering along with the enthusiastic audience.

Catching a Movie at Theatres:

Ximending is also known for its cinemas, and I couldn't resist catching a movie at one of the popular theaters. The experience was unique, with some theaters offering themed interiors and a range of local and international films. It was a great way to unwind and immerse myself in Taiwanese pop culture.

Connecting with Locals:

One of the highlights of my Ximending adventure was the warmth and friendliness of the locals. Whether I was asking for directions or simply chatting with street vendors, the locals made me feel right at home. Their genuine hospitality added a special touch to my experience.

Hidden Gems and Street Art:

While exploring Ximending's alleys, I stumbled upon hidden gems like indie cafes and art spaces that oozed creativity. The district's vibrant street art adorned walls and buildings, adding a unique charm to every corner.

Conclusion:

My first-time experience in Ximending was nothing short of extraordinary. This urban playground offers an immersive blend of culture, entertainment, and culinary delights. From shopping to street food adventures and connecting with locals, Ximending left me with cherished memories that will forever hold a place in my heart. I can't wait for you to experience the magic of Ximending for yourself. Happy travels, and embrace the vibrant spirit of Taipei's dynamic district!

Shilin

Welcome to Shilin, a dynamic and vibrant district in Taipei that has so much to offer. As an insider who has spent countless hours wandering through its bustling streets, savoring its delectable street food, and uncovering its hidden gems, I'm excited to share my personal experiences with you. So, let's dive into the heart of Shilin together and uncover the secrets of this lively neighborhood!

Arriving in Shilin:

The moment you step foot in Shilin, you'll be greeted by a lively atmosphere and a palpable sense of energy. The district is renowned for its iconic Shilin Night Market, but there's so much more to explore beyond that. Get ready to be captivated by the colorful chaos and the myriad of sights and sounds that make Shilin unique.

Shilin Night Market Extravaganza:

The heartbeat of Shilin is undoubtedly its famous night market. As the sun sets, the market comes alive with a kaleidoscope of lights, enticing aromas, and the buzz of eager shoppers. This is the place to indulge in an array of street food delights, from the irresistible stinky tofu to the sizzling pepper buns and the refreshing shaved ice desserts.

Hidden Treasures:

Beyond the bustling main streets lie hidden treasures waiting to be discovered. Explore the narrow alleys and you'll stumble upon charming cafes, quaint boutiques, and local shops that offer unique and eclectic finds. Shilin is a treasure trove for those who enjoy exploring off the beaten path.

Cultural Encounters:

Shilin's cultural tapestry is a beautiful blend of tradition and modernity. You'll encounter ancient temples juxtaposed with contemporary street art, creating a harmonious fusion of the old and the new. Be sure to pay a visit to the historic Cixian Temple and immerse yourself in its serene ambiance.

Embracing the Nightlife:

As the night deepens, Shilin's nightlife comes to life. The district offers a range of entertainment options, from karaoke bars and pubs to chic lounges. Join the locals in celebrating the night, and you'll be treated to an unforgettable experience.

Meeting the Locals:

The people of Shilin are known for their warmth and hospitality. Don't be afraid to strike up a conversation with a vendor at the night market or share a smile with a passerby. Connecting with the locals will not only enrich your experience but also leave you with heartwarming memories.

Ease of Transportation:

Getting around Shilin is a breeze, thanks to its accessible transportation options. The Shilin MRT station and well-connected bus routes make it convenient to navigate through the district and explore other parts of Taipei.

Conclusion:

There you have it—my insider's perspective on Shilin, a district filled with culinary delights, cultural encounters, and hidden treasures waiting to be uncovered. Whether you're savoring the flavors of the night market, immersing yourself in the local culture, or exploring the district's lesser-known corners, Shilin promises an unforgettable adventure. Embrace the spirit of exploration, indulge in the vibrant atmosphere, and let the charm of Shilin captivate your heart. Happy exploring in this dynamic neighborhood of Taipei!

Zhongshan

Welcome to Zhongshan, a district in Taipei that's brimming with history, culture, and hidden gems. As an insider who has explored the nooks and crannies of this captivating neighborhood, I'm thrilled to share my personal experiences and tips to make your Zhongshan adventure truly special. Let's embark on this journey together!

A Walk through History:

Zhongshan is steeped in history, and a walk through its streets is like stepping back in time. The district is named after Dr. Sun Yat-sen, the founding father of modern China, and you'll find historical landmarks and monuments dedicated to him throughout the area. Exploring these historical sites offers a glimpse into Taiwan's past and its connection to Chinese history.

Cultural Enclaves:

One of the highlights of Zhongshan is its cultural diversity. The district is home to vibrant cultural enclaves, including Little Tokyo and Little Manila, where you can experience the influence of different cultures through food, events, and celebrations. These enclaves offer a unique perspective on Taipei's multicultural identity.

Fashion and Shopping:

Zhongshan is a fashion lover's paradise, with trendy boutiques and chic shopping streets. Explore the bustling Zhongshan Metro Mall for a wide selection of stylish clothing and accessories. The district's fashion scene caters to all tastes, from contemporary to vintage, making it a great place to find your unique style.

Culinary Delights:

Zhongshan boasts a diverse food scene, from traditional Taiwanese dishes to international cuisine. Venture into the local eateries and night markets to savor mouthwatering delicacies. Don't forget to try the iconic beef noodle soup, a must-try dish in Taipei!

Art and Creativity:

Creativity flows through Zhongshan's veins, and you'll find art spaces and galleries that showcase local talent. Art lovers can visit the Huashan 1914 Creative Park, a vibrant hub of artistic expression. The district's artistic atmosphere is sure to inspire and captivate you.

Serene Parks and Gardens:

Amidst the urban buzz, Zhongshan offers serene parks and gardens where you can escape and unwind. The Lin An Tai Historical House and Museum, set within a tranquil garden, is a hidden gem that offers a peaceful retreat from the city's hustle and bustle.

Local Connections:

One of the most enriching aspects of exploring Zhongshan is connecting with the locals. Whether you strike up a conversation at a café or join a community event, the warmth and friendliness of the people will make you feel at home in this bustling district.

Accessible Transportation:

Zhongshan is well-connected with Taipei's transportation system, making it easy to explore other parts of the city. The Zhongshan MRT station and nearby bus routes ensure convenient access to various attractions and destinations.

Conclusion:

There you have it—my insider's guide to Zhongshan, a district filled with history, culture, and creative energy. From historical landmarks to cultural enclaves and serene gardens, Zhongshan offers a delightful fusion of past and present. As you venture into this captivating neighborhood, I hope my tips help you uncover the hidden gems and unique experiences that await you. Embrace the spirit of exploration, connect with the locals, and immerse yourself in the vibrant tapestry of Zhongshan. Happy adventures in Taipei's captivating district!

Daan

Welcome to Daan, one of Taipei's most diverse and vibrant districts. As an insider who has explored Daan's charming streets, savored its delectable cuisine, and immersed myself in its local culture, I'm excited to share my personal experiences with you. So, let's embark on a virtual journey through Daan and discover the hidden gems that make this district so special!

Embracing the Diversity:

Daan is a melting pot of cultures, attracting residents from all walks of life. As you explore its streets, you'll witness the harmonious blend of modernity and tradition. From chic boutiques to ancient temples, Daan effortlessly weaves together the old and the new, creating a unique charm that captivates all who visit.

Shopping Paradise:

Fashion enthusiasts will find themselves in paradise when they step into Daan's shopping scene. The district boasts a diverse array of shopping options, from luxury brands to trendy local boutiques. Whether you're hunting for high-end fashion or searching for unique pieces, Daan has something for every style and taste.

Foodie Haven:

Prepare your taste buds for an adventure, as Daan is a haven for foodies. From bustling night markets to hip cafes and traditional eateries, you'll find an endless array of culinary delights. Don't miss out on trying the famous Din Tai Fung soup dumplings or savoring a refreshing bubble tea from its birthplace.

Serene Parks and Retreats:

Daan offers tranquil escapes in its serene parks and gardens. Daan Forest Park, the largest green oasis in Taipei, is a perfect spot for a leisurely stroll or a relaxing picnic. Breathe in the fresh air and recharge amidst nature's embrace.

Art and Creativity:

Art aficionados will be delighted to discover Daan's creative scene. The district houses art galleries, design studios, and independent art spaces that showcase local talent. Be sure to explore the eclectic art installations and immerse yourself in the district's artistic spirit.

Cultural Discoveries:

Daan's cultural diversity is reflected in its places of worship and historical landmarks. Visit the beautiful Fuyang Temple or the tranquil Jianguo Jade Market to experience the district's spiritual side. You'll encounter a blend of ancient traditions and contemporary practices that reflect the essence of Daan's identity.

Easy Connectivity:

Getting around Daan is easy and convenient. The district is well-connected with Taipei's transportation system, making it effortless to explore other parts of the city. Hop on the MRT or take a leisurely walk to discover more of what Taipei has to offer.

Local Interactions:

Interacting with locals in Daan is a delightful experience. The residents are known for their friendly nature and welcoming attitude. Strike up a conversation with a shop owner, join a local event, or simply share a smile with a passerby to feel the warmth of Daan's community.

Conclusion:

There you have it—my insider's guide to Daan, a district that embraces diversity, creativity, and culinary delights. From fashion and food to art and cultural encounters, Daan promises an enriching experience for every traveler. Embrace the vibrant spirit of this district, connect with the locals, and allow the charm of Daan to captivate your heart. Happy exploring in Taipei's diverse and lively neighborhood!

Beitou

Welcome to Beitou, a hidden gem nestled in the northern part of Taipei. As an insider who has explored Beitou's tranquil hot springs, ventured through its lush greenery, and experienced its cultural treasures, I'm thrilled to share my personal experiences with you. So, let's embark on a virtual journey through Beitou and uncover the natural wonders and cultural delights that await!

The Gateway to Nature:

Beitou is renowned for its natural beauty and hot springs, making it a serene escape from the hustle and bustle of the city. As you enter this oasis, you'll be greeted by a sense of tranquility and a lush landscape that beckons you to unwind and immerse yourself in the beauty of nature.

Hot Springs Haven:

The hot springs! Beitou is famous for its therapeutic geothermal waters, and no trip here is complete without a rejuvenating hot spring experience. Whether you indulge in a public bathhouse or opt for a private hot spring resort, the healing waters will soothe your body and soul.

Beitou Hot Springs Museum:

For a touch of history and culture, don't miss the Beitou Hot Springs Museum. This charming building was once a Japanese public bathhouse and now serves as a cultural and historical landmark. It's a fascinating glimpse into Beitou's rich hot spring heritage.

Lush Green Parks:

Beitou is a paradise for nature lovers, and its parks are a testament to that. Beitou Park offers a serene environment with walking trails and picturesque scenery. Beitou Thermal Valley, also known as Hell Valley, is an awe-inspiring geothermal attraction that showcases the power of nature.

Cultural Gems:

Beitou is dotted with cultural gems. The Ketagalan Cultural Center offers insights into the local indigenous culture, while the Plum Garden, once the residence of a renowned Taiwanese writer, immerses you in literary history.

Hot Spring Cuisine:

As you explore Beitou, don't forget to indulge in the local hot spring cuisine. Many restaurants and tea houses offer dishes that are steamed using the natural hot spring steam, resulting in flavorful and healthy meals.

Ease of Accessibility:

Despite its tranquil atmosphere, Beitou is easily accessible via the MRT, making it a convenient day trip from Taipei. The journey itself is a scenic delight, passing through lush landscapes and glimpses of the beautiful Tamsui River.

Embrace the Relaxing Vibes:

Beitou's essence lies in its relaxing vibes. Slow down, take a leisurely walk, soak in the hot springs, and let the peaceful ambiance rejuvenate your spirit. It's the perfect getaway for those seeking a peaceful retreat.

Conclusion:

There you have it—my insider's guide to Beitou, a haven of nature, hot springs, and cultural treasures. Whether you're immersing yourself in the healing waters, exploring the lush parks, or delving into the district's rich history, Beitou promises an enchanting experience for every traveler. Embrace the tranquility, savor the local cuisine, and let the allure of Beitou captivate your heart. Happy adventures in this picturesque corner of Taipei!

Wanhua

Welcome to Wanhua, the oldest district in Taipei, brimming with history, culture, and fascinating experiences. As an insider who has wandered through Wanhua's ancient streets, discovered its hidden gems, and immersed myself in its vibrant atmosphere, I'm excited to share my personal insights with you. So, let's set off on an insider's journey through Wanhua and uncover the allure of this captivating district!

A Glimpse of History:

Wanhua is a living testament to Taipei's past, with a history that dates back centuries. The district is dotted with historical landmarks and temples that offer a glimpse into its rich cultural heritage. As you explore Wanhua's ancient streets, you'll be transported back in time, surrounded by centuries-old architecture and the echoes of a bygone era.

The Iconic Longshan Temple:

No trip to Wanhua is complete without visiting the iconic Longshan Temple. This centuries-old temple is a spiritual center and a cultural treasure of Taipei.

Step inside to witness the beautiful architecture, intricate carvings, and immerse yourself in the spiritual ambiance.

Shopping and Street Delights:

Wanhua is a bustling district with a vibrant street scene. From the vibrant night market to local shops and boutiques, you'll find a wide array of goods and street food delights to tantalize your senses. Savor local snacks, explore the bustling market stalls, and soak in the lively atmosphere.

Huaxi Street Night Market:

The lively Huaxi Street Night Market, also known as Snake Alley, is a unique and iconic part of Wanhua. While it may have a somewhat controversial history, the night market offers a glimpse into Taipei's past and is a hub of diverse culinary experiences. Enjoy the lively atmosphere and try out the local delicacies.

Hidden Art and Culture:

Beyond the bustling streets, Wanhua harbors hidden art and cultural treasures. Explore art studios, galleries, and independent spaces where local artists showcase their creativity. The district's artistic soul is waiting to be discovered by those who venture off the beaten path.

Temples and Traditions:

Aside from the famous Longshan Temple, Wanhua is home to several other traditional temples that hold significant cultural value. Pay a visit to Bopiliao Historic Block, where the old and the new converge, showcasing Wanhua's cultural heritage.

Transportation and Accessibility:

Wanhua is well-connected to Taipei's transportation network, making it easily accessible for travelers. The MRT and bus routes ensure convenient travel, allowing you to explore the rest of Taipei with ease.

Local Hospitality:

One of the most endearing aspects of Wanhua is the hospitality of its residents. The locals are warm, friendly, and often eager to share stories about the district's history and traditions. Engaging with them will enrich your experience and leave you with heartwarming memories.

Conclusion:

There you have it—my insider's guide to Wanhua, a district steeped in history, culture, and local charm. From exploring ancient temples to savoring local delights at the night market, Wanhua promises an enriching journey into Taipei's past and present. Embrace the district's cultural heritage, connect with the locals, and let the magic of Wanhua captivate your heart. Happy adventures in this historical gem of Taipei!

Top Taipei Attractions

Taipei 101

Hey there, first-time traveler! Welcome to Taipei 101, the towering icon of Taipei and a must-visit destination for every adventurer. As an insider with a funny tale to tell, let me share my personal experience with you. Get ready to laugh and enjoy the ride as we dive into my comical encounter at Taipei 101!

The Towering Impression:

So, picture this—I arrived at Taipei 101, looking up at its grandeur, and my jaw dropped like a cartoon character! It was so massive that I felt like a tiny ant standing next to it. My friends and I couldn't help but joke about how this skyscraper could practically touch the sky!

Observatory Adventures:

We decided to venture up to the observatory decks to take in the breathtaking views. But as we stood in the elevator, I realized I had a mild fear of heights. My friends were teasing me about being a scaredy-cat, and I tried to play it cool, but my heart was pounding like crazy!

The Nervous Laughter:

As we ascended, the elevator windows offered glimpses of the ground far below, and my nerves kicked in. My friends were excitedly talking about the view, but all I could manage were nervous laughs and comments like, "Wow, what a great cityscape!" I didn't dare look down!

The Windy Surprise:

Once we reached the indoor observatory, I thought I was safe from the height anxiety. But oh boy, was I in for a surprise! The wind outside was unexpectedly strong, and I was clinging to the railing like it was a lifeline. My friends found it hilarious, of course, and kept joking that the wind might blow me away!

A Buffet of Laughter:

To calm my nerves, we decided to have a meal at the dining area on the observatory floor. The buffet spread was amazing, and I was looking forward to enjoying the delicious food. But fate had other plans. As I reached for a plate, I accidentally dropped it, and it made such a loud noise that everyone turned to look at me. Cue the embarrassed laughter!

Souvenir Shopping Mishap:

To top it off, when we went souvenir shopping, I got so excited that I ended up knocking over a display of cute Taipei 101 keychains. The shopkeeper gave me a playful scolding, and my friends couldn't stop laughing. It was a moment of pure clumsiness!

Fond Memories:

Despite my funny little mishaps, I had an incredible time at Taipei 101. The view was breathtaking, the experience unforgettable, and the laughter shared with my friends made it even more special. We still reminisce about that day and have a good laugh whenever we talk about my quirky adventures.

Conclusion:

There you have it—the story of my first-time traveler funny experience at Taipei 101. Despite my fear of heights and a few clumsy mishaps, the laughter and memories I made that day will stay with me forever. So, if you find yourself nervous or unsure on your first visit, don't worry—we all have our funny moments! Embrace the experience, have a good laugh, and enjoy every bit of your Taipei 101 adventure. Happy travels, and may your trip be filled with memorable moments and plenty of humor!

National Palace Museum

Welcome to the National Palace Museum, a treasure trove of Chinese culture and heritage. As an insider who has wandered through its hallowed halls and marveled at its priceless artifacts, I'm thrilled to share my personal experiences with you. So, let's embark on a virtual journey through the National Palace Museum and uncover the wonders that lie within this cultural gem!

A World of Treasures:

The National Palace Museum houses an extensive collection of over 700,000 Chinese artifacts, spanning thousands of years of history. As you step inside, you'll be transported back in time, surrounded by an incredible array of ancient art, calligraphy, ceramics, jade carvings, and more. Each piece tells a unique story of China's rich cultural legacy.

The Main Exhibitions:

The museum's main exhibitions are a true feast for the eyes and mind. The rare artifacts on display offer an intimate glimpse into the lives of emperors, scholars, and everyday people from different dynasties. The exquisite craftsmanship and attention to detail will leave you in awe of China's artistic heritage.

Treasures from Forbidden City:

Many of the artifacts in the museum were once part of the imperial collection in Beijing's Forbidden City. During times of war and political changes, these treasures were moved to Taiwan, safeguarding them from potential destruction. It's a fascinating journey of how these cultural gems found their way to their current home.

Special Exhibitions:

The museum also hosts special exhibitions that showcase specific themes or collections. These exhibitions provide a fresh perspective on different aspects of Chinese culture and art. Be sure to check the museum's schedule to see if there are any special exhibitions during your visit.

Interactive Learning:

The National Palace Museum offers interactive learning experiences that are both fun and educational. You can participate in workshops, calligraphy classes, and even try on traditional clothing. These activities add an immersive element to your visit and bring history and culture to life.

Taiwanese Cultural Heritage:

The museum also celebrates Taiwan's unique cultural heritage, showcasing artifacts that are deeply rooted in the island's history. It's a wonderful opportunity to appreciate the richness of Taiwanese culture and its connections to the broader Chinese heritage.

Breathtaking Gardens:

Beyond the exhibits, don't miss the museum's beautiful gardens and landscapes. Stroll through the serene surroundings, and you'll feel a sense of tranquility that complements the cultural journey inside the museum.

Accessibility and Transportation:

The National Palace Museum is easily accessible via public transportation, and the convenient shuttle service from central Taipei makes it a breeze to reach. Plan your trip accordingly, and you'll have ample time to explore and appreciate the museum's treasures.

Conclusion:

There you have it—my insider's guide to the National Palace Museum, a treasure house of Chinese culture and art. From the ancient artifacts to the interactive learning experiences, the museum promises an enriching journey through China's history and heritage. Embrace the artistic legacy, immerse yourself in the stories of the past, and let the wonder of the National Palace Museum leave you with cherished memories. Happy exploration in this cultural haven of Taipei!

Chiang Kai-shek Memorial Hall

Welcome to the Chiang Kai-shek Memorial Hall, a significant landmark and a symbol of Taiwan's history and culture. As an insider who has wandered through its majestic grounds and delved into its historical significance, I'm thrilled to share my personal experiences with you. So, let's embark on a virtual journey through the Chiang Kai-shek Memorial Hall and uncover the fascinating stories it holds!

A Grand Monument:

The Chiang Kai-shek Memorial Hall stands tall and imposing, surrounded by lush gardens and a tranquil pond. The sight of this grand monument will leave you in awe of its architectural magnificence.

Guarded by Lions:

As you approach the memorial, you'll notice the majestic lions flanking the entrance. These stone guardians add a touch of regal charm and pay homage to traditional Chinese symbolism.

The Elegant Staircase:

Climbing the grand staircase to reach the main hall is a memorable experience. The sweeping staircase seems to lead you to another era, evoking a sense of reverence and importance.

The Main Hall:

The main hall is the heart of the memorial, and it houses a massive bronze statue of General Chiang Kai-shek. The serene atmosphere inside the hall and the soft lighting create a respectful ambiance.

Changing of the Guard:

Don't miss the impressive Changing of the Guard ceremony that takes place hourly. The precision and discipline of the guards are truly captivating to watch, and it adds a touch of ceremonial splendor to the memorial.

Exquisite Artifacts:

The memorial hall also displays an intriguing collection of historical artifacts, including documents, photographs, and personal belongings of Chiang Kai-shek. These exhibits offer a glimpse into the life and legacy of the prominent figure.

A Place of Reflection:

The memorial hall is not just a monument; it's also a place of reflection and contemplation. The surrounding gardens and the peaceful atmosphere make it an ideal spot to pause and gather your thoughts.

Lively Gatherings:

The square in front of the memorial is often a hub of activity. You might stumble upon cultural events, concerts, or even colorful celebrations, where locals come together to celebrate Taiwan's heritage.

Epicenter of History:

The Chiang Kai-shek Memorial Hall is a historical epicenter, reflecting Taiwan's journey from its past to the present. It's a place that holds deep meaning for the locals, and you'll witness a sense of reverence among visitors paying their respects.

Conclusion:

There you have it—my insider's guide to the Chiang Kai-shek Memorial Hall, a captivating blend of history, culture, and serenity. As you wander through its impressive halls and peaceful gardens, I hope you feel a connection to Taiwan's rich past and cultural heritage. Embrace the significance, appreciate the grandeur, and let the Chiang Kai-shek Memorial Hall leave an indelible mark on your heart. Happy exploration in this iconic Taipei landmark!

Longshan Temple

Welcome to Longshan Temple, a place of spiritual tranquility and cultural significance. As an insider who has visited this historic temple and experienced its profound ambiance, I'm thrilled to share my personal insights with you. So, let's embark on a virtual journey through Longshan Temple and discover the tales and traditions that make it a cherished treasure of Taipei!

A Temple of History:

Longshan Temple is steeped in history, dating back to its construction in 1738. Its rich heritage and architectural beauty make it one of the oldest and most revered temples in Taipei.

An Intricate Facade:

As you approach the temple's entrance, you'll be captivated by the intricate facade adorned with traditional Chinese designs and intricate carvings. The vibrant colors and ornate details add to the temple's allure.

A Gateway to Spirituality:

Stepping inside Longshan Temple is like entering another world—a realm of spirituality and devotion. The atmosphere is serene, and the aroma of burning incense fills the air, creating a sense of peace and reverence.

The Melodious Chants:

Amidst the soft whispers of prayers, you'll hear the soothing sound of chanting and the rhythmic rhythm of temple bells. The chants add a melodic touch to the spiritual experience and enhance the temple's divine aura.

Blessings and Offerings:

Witnessing locals offering incense, flowers, and other offerings to the deities is a beautiful sight. The act of making wishes and seeking blessings is an integral part of the temple's traditions, and you may be inspired to partake in this ancient ritual.

A Tapestry of Deities:

Longshan Temple is dedicated to various deities, each representing different aspects of life. As you explore the temple's different halls, you'll encounter a diverse tapestry of gods and goddesses.

Cultural Encounters:

The temple's courtyard often hosts cultural events and celebrations that offer a glimpse into Taiwan's traditional arts and customs. It's a delightful opportunity to immerse yourself in the local culture.

A Place of Community:

Longshan Temple is not just a place of worship; it's also a community hub. Locals gather here to socialize, seek guidance, and participate in cultural events, creating a strong sense of camaraderie.

Timeless Resilience:

Throughout its long history, Longshan Temple has withstood challenges such as natural disasters and wars. Its resilience and enduring significance to the local community exemplify its importance in Taiwanese culture.

Conclusion:

There you have it—my insider's guide to Longshan Temple, a haven of spirituality, culture, and tradition. As you explore its sacred halls, absorb the ambiance, and witness the devotion of the worshippers, you'll feel a profound connection to

Taiwan's cultural roots. Embrace the spiritual serenity, appreciate the historical legacy, and let the captivating Longshan Temple leave an everlasting impression on your heart. Happy exploration and may your visit be filled with profound moments of tranquility!

Elephant Mountain

Welcome to Elephant Mountain, a nature lover's paradise and a popular spot for outdoor enthusiasts in Taipei. As an insider who has hiked up this scenic trail, marveled at its breathtaking views, and relished the sense of achievement at the top, I'm thrilled to share my personal insights with you. So, let's embark on a virtual journey up Elephant Mountain and uncover the wonders that await!

Nature's Haven:

Elephant Mountain is a lush oasis nestled in the heart of Taipei. The trail takes you away from the bustling city, and as you start your ascent, you'll be surrounded by the beauty of nature—tall trees, chirping birds, and the gentle rustling of leaves.

Hiking Adventure:

Get ready for an exciting hiking adventure! The trail is well-maintained and relatively easy to follow, but be prepared for some stairs and steep sections. Don't worry, though; the rewarding views at the top are well worth the effort!

Scenic Pit Stops:

As you hike, you'll come across several viewpoints where you can pause, catch your breath, and soak in the picturesque scenery. These little pit stops allow you to enjoy the journey and appreciate the natural beauty around you.

Taipei 101 Viewpoint:

One of the highlights of Elephant Mountain is the famous Taipei 101 viewpoint. When you reach the top, you'll be treated to a jaw-dropping panoramic view of Taipei's skyline, with the iconic Taipei 101 soaring majestically in the distance.

Sunset Spectacle:

For a truly magical experience, consider hiking up Elephant Mountain in the late afternoon to catch the sunset. Watching the sun dip below the horizon, casting hues of orange and pink over the city, is a sight you won't soon forget.

Nighttime Cityscape:

If you're up for a nighttime adventure, head up Elephant Mountain after dark. The city lights twinkling below create a mesmerizing urban canvas, giving you a whole new perspective of Taipei at night.

Pack Your Essentials:

Before you start your hike, make sure to pack essentials like water, comfortable shoes, and sunscreen. And don't forget your camera—you'll want to capture the breathtaking views along the way!

A Sense of Achievement:

Reaching the top of Elephant Mountain fills you with a sense of accomplishment and awe. It's a moment to celebrate conquering the trail and appreciating the stunning natural and urban landscapes that Taipei has to offer.

Share the Moment:

Whether you hike alone or with friends, the experience of Elephant Mountain is best shared. Take a group photo at the top to commemorate the journey and create lasting memories with your fellow adventurers.

Conclusion:

There you have it—my insider's guide to Elephant Mountain, a nature retreat and a hiker's delight in Taipei. From the refreshing hike through lush greenery to the awe-inspiring views of the city, Elephant Mountain promises a memorable experience for every adventurer. Embrace the natural beauty, savor the stunning vistas, and let the spirit of exploration guide you as you hike this incredible trail. Happy trekking and may your journey up Elephant Mountain be filled with unforgettable moments and a deep appreciation for Taipei's natural wonders!

Maokong Gondola

Welcome to the Maokong Gondola, a breathtaking journey that takes you from the bustling city to the tranquil tea plantations of Maokong. As an insider who has ridden these suspended cabins, marveled at the scenic vistas, and embraced the serenity of Maokong, I'm thrilled to share my personal experiences with you. So, let's embark on a virtual adventure through the Maokong Gondola and uncover the delights that await!

Aerial Excursion:

The Maokong Gondola is not just a mode of transportation; it's an aerial excursion that offers captivating views of Taipei's landscape. As you board the suspended cabin, you'll feel a rush of excitement knowing that you're about to embark on a memorable journey.

Spectacular Scenery:

As the gondola glides smoothly above the treetops, you'll be treated to stunning panoramas of Taipei's urban jungle, distant mountains, and glimpses of the serene Maokong tea plantations below.

Tea Plantation Retreat:

The journey takes you to Maokong, a charming tea-growing region with lush terraced fields and quaint teahouses. It's the perfect escape from the city's hustle and a chance to immerse yourself in the tranquility of nature.

Tea House Delights:

At Maokong, don't miss the opportunity to visit one of the traditional teahouses. Here, you can savor aromatic Taiwanese teas, expertly prepared and served by tea connoisseurs. It's an authentic experience that will delight your taste buds and soothe your soul.

Relaxing Ambiance:

Whether you choose to sit indoors or enjoy your tea on a terrace with a view, the teahouses exude a relaxing ambiance. The gentle breeze, chirping birds, and the aroma of tea create a serene atmosphere that complements the tea-drinking ritual.

Nature Walks:

For nature enthusiasts, Maokong offers walking trails that lead you through the tea plantations and surrounding greenery. It's a delightful way to connect with nature and enjoy the natural beauty of the area.

Sunset Magic:

If you time your visit right, witnessing the sunset from Maokong is pure magic. As the sun dips below the horizon, the golden hues cast a warm glow over the landscape, making it a perfect moment for a memorable photograph.

Cable Car Return:

As you bid farewell to Maokong and board the gondola for the return journey, take a moment to reflect on the experiences and memories you've gathered on this enchanting ride.

Accessibility:

The Maokong Gondola is easily accessible via public transportation, making it a convenient excursion from Taipei. It's a popular attraction, so plan your visit accordingly to avoid long queues during peak times.

Conclusion:

There you have it—my insider's guide to the Maokong Gondola, an aerial journey to the tea plantations of Maokong. From the spectacular views to the serene teahouses, this experience promises an enchanting adventure for every traveler. Embrace the scenic vistas, indulge in tea culture, and let the Maokong Gondola and its tranquil surroundings leave an indelible mark on your heart. Happy soaring through the skies and may your visit to

Maokong be filled with unforgettable moments and a deep appreciation for Taipei's natural wonders!

Embracing Culture and Arts

Taipei Fine Arts Museum

Welcome to the Taipei Fine Arts Museum, a captivating haven for contemporary art lovers in Taipei. As an insider who has explored its artistic wonders, attended inspiring exhibitions, and experienced the creative vibe within its walls, I'm excited to share my personal insights with you. So, let's embark on a virtual tour through the Taipei Fine Arts Museum and immerse ourselves in the world of contemporary art!

Artistic Architecture:

The Taipei Fine Arts Museum is a masterpiece in itself. Its modern architecture stands out, with unique geometric shapes and a glass exterior that lets natural light filter in, creating a dynamic space for art to shine.

Curated Exhibitions:

As you step inside the museum, you'll be greeted by an ever-changing landscape of curated exhibitions. The museum hosts a diverse range of contemporary artworks from both local and international artists, showcasing various styles, themes, and artistic expressions.

Inspiring Artistic Journeys:

Exploring the exhibitions is like taking a journey through the minds of artists. Each artwork has a story to tell, a message to convey, or an emotion to evoke. It's a place where you can delve into the creative realms of different cultures and perspectives.

Interactive Installations:

The Taipei Fine Arts Museum often features interactive installations that engage visitors in unique ways. From multimedia displays to immersive experiences, these installations bridge the gap between the art and the audience, creating a dynamic and unforgettable encounter.

Local Art Community:

The museum plays an integral role in Taipei's art scene, fostering a vibrant local art community. It hosts events, workshops, and art talks, bringing artists and art enthusiasts together to exchange ideas and inspire one another.

Art Appreciation Spaces:

Throughout the museum, you'll find cozy corners and seating areas, where you can take a moment to appreciate the art and reflect on your artistic journey. It's a space that encourages contemplation and introspection.

Café and Bookstore:

Don't miss the museum's café and bookstore. It's a perfect spot to relax, enjoy a cup of coffee, and discuss art with fellow visitors. The bookstore offers a wide selection of art-related publications and souvenirs to take home.

Events and Workshops:

Keep an eye on the museum's schedule for upcoming events and workshops. Participating in art-related activities can deepen your appreciation for creativity and enhance your overall experience at the museum.

Accessibility:

Insider: The Taipei Fine Arts Museum is easily accessible via public transportation, making it convenient for art lovers to visit. Plan your trip, and allow ample time to explore and absorb the artistic wonders it has to offer.

Conclusion:

There you have it—my insider's guide to the Taipei Fine Arts Museum, a captivating space that celebrates contemporary art and creativity. From the inspiring exhibitions to the interactive installations, this museum promises an enriching journey for every art enthusiast. Embrace the artistic expressions, immerse yourself in the creative ambiance, and let the Taipei Fine Arts Museum leave a lasting impression on your artistic soul.

Happy exploration, and may your visit be filled with profound moments of artistic inspiration!

Huashan 1914 Creative Park

Welcome to Huashan 1914 Creative Park, an artistic and cultural hub in the heart of Taipei. As an insider who has wandered through its eclectic galleries, attended vibrant events, and embraced the creative energy within its historic walls, I'm thrilled to share my personal insights with you. So, let's embark on a virtual journey through Huashan 1914 Creative Park and dive into the dynamic world of art and culture!

A Historic Transformation:

Huashan 1914 Creative Park was once an industrial complex dating back to the Japanese colonial period. Today, it has been beautifully transformed into a creative and cultural space, preserving its historical charm while fostering modern artistic endeavors.

Artistic Galleries and Exhibitions:

As you step into Huashan, you'll find yourself surrounded by a myriad of galleries showcasing contemporary art, photography, design, and more. The exhibitions are ever-changing, ensuring there's always something new and exciting to discover.

Creative Boutiques:

The park is also home to quirky boutiques and craft shops offering unique creations by local artists and designers. From handmade jewelry to artistic stationery, these boutiques are a treasure trove for finding one-of-a-kind souvenirs.

Cultural Events and Festivals:

Huashan is a hub of cultural events and festivals throughout the year. From art festivals and music performances to film screenings and creative workshops, there's always a buzz of excitement in the air.

Live Performances and Theaters:

If you're a fan of performing arts, you're in for a treat! Huashan often hosts live performances, theater productions, and dance shows that showcase the diverse talent of Taiwan's performing arts scene.

Cafés and Food Stalls:

When you need a break from exploring, the park's cafés and food stalls offer a delightful respite. Grab a cup of freshly brewed coffee or sample delicious street food while soaking in the park's vibrant ambiance.

Relaxing Courtyards:

Huashan boasts charming courtyards and open spaces, providing a serene setting to sit, relax, and people-watch. It's a perfect spot to take a breather and absorb the creativity that surrounds you.

Artistic Workshops:

Check out the schedule for artistic workshops and classes offered at Huashan. Whether you're interested in painting, photography, or crafts, these workshops provide a hands-on experience for budding artists.

Night Markets and Flea Markets:

On selected evenings, Huashan transforms into a lively night market or flea market, where you can browse through an array of handmade crafts, vintage finds, and artisanal goods.

Accessibility:

Huashan 1914 Creative Park is easily accessible by public transportation, making it a convenient destination for culture seekers in Taipei. Plan your visit to coincide with events or exhibitions that pique your interest.

Conclusion:

There you have it—my insider's guide to Huashan 1914 Creative Park, a vibrant cultural oasis in Taipei. From the artistic galleries to the lively events, this creative hub promises an enriching journey for every culture enthusiast. Embrace the artistic expressions, immerse yourself in the cultural festivities, and let Huashan 1914 Creative Park leave a lasting impression on your artistic soul. Happy exploration, and may your visit be filled with unforgettable moments of artistic inspiration and cultural delight!

National Theater and Concert Hall

Welcome to the National Theater and Concert Hall, a cultural gem nestled in the heart of Taipei. As an insider who has immersed myself in the artistic wonders of this iconic venue, attended breathtaking performances, and cherished the history it holds, I'm excited to share my personal insights with you. So, let's embark on a virtual journey through the majestic halls of the National Theater and Concert Hall and discover the world of arts and performances!

A Cultural Landmark:

The National Theater and Concert Hall stand tall as a cultural landmark in Taipei. These architectural masterpieces are not only venues for artistic performances but also symbols of Taiwan's commitment to preserving and celebrating its rich cultural heritage.

Grand Architecture:

The grandeur of the National Theater and Concert Hall is awe-inspiring. The traditional Chinese architectural elements combined with modern touches create a harmonious and majestic setting, fitting for the world-class performances that take place within.

The National Theater:

The National Theater is a treasure trove of traditional performances, such as Chinese opera, dance dramas, and classical theater. The stage comes alive with vibrant colors, intricate costumes, and masterful storytelling that transport the audience to another era.

The Concert Hall:

The Concert Hall is a haven for music enthusiasts. Its acoustics are meticulously designed to ensure the most immersive auditory experience. From classical symphonies to contemporary concerts, the Concert Hall hosts a diverse range of musical performances that captivate the soul.

Star-Studded Performances:

The National Theater and Concert Hall often host performances by world-renowned artists and local talents alike. Watching virtuosos and maestros grace the stage is a once-in-a-lifetime experience that leaves a lasting impression.

Cultural Festivals and Events:

Throughout the year, the National Theater and Concert Hall come alive with cultural festivals, arts showcases, and special events. These celebrations offer a kaleidoscope of artistic expressions and provide a deeper understanding of Taiwanese culture.

Artistic Workshops and Exhibitions:

The venue isn't just for performances; it's also a hub of artistic exploration. Art workshops and exhibitions provide opportunities for aspiring artists to learn from the masters and showcase their creativity to a diverse audience.

Cafés and Cultural Ambiance:

Take a break at the cafés within the complex and soak in the cultural ambiance. The venue's serene courtyards and open spaces create a perfect setting for relaxation and contemplation after an inspiring performance.

Accessibility:

Getting to the National Theater and Concert Hall is convenient, thanks to its central location in Taipei. It's easily accessible by public transportation, making it a must-visit destination for culture enthusiasts.

Conclusion:

There you have it—my insider's guide to the National Theater and Concert Hall, a cultural treasure trove in Taipei. From the breathtaking performances to the majestic architecture, this venue promises an enriching journey for every culture lover. Embrace the artistic expressions, immerse yourself in the cultural festivities, and let the National Theater and Concert Hall ignite your passion for the arts. Happy exploration, and may your visit be filled with unforgettable moments of cultural wonder and artistic inspiration!

Traditional Taiwanese Puppetry

Welcome to the enchanting world of Traditional Taiwanese Puppetry, a captivating art form that has delighted audiences for centuries. As an insider who has witnessed the intricacies of puppetry performances, marveled at the craftsmanship of the puppets, and embraced the cultural heritage they represent, I'm thrilled to share my personal insights with you. So, let's embark on a virtual journey through the mesmerizing realm of Traditional Taiwanese Puppetry!

A Rich Cultural Heritage:

Traditional Taiwanese Puppetry is deeply rooted in Taiwanese culture and history. Its origins can be traced back to ancient religious rituals and folk celebrations, making it a cherished art form passed down through generations.

Master Puppeteers:

Behind the scenes of every puppetry performance are skilled puppeteers who breathe life into these intricate wooden figures. These masters of their craft undergo rigorous training and spend years honing their skills to bring the puppets to life on the stage.

Exquisite Puppet Craftsmanship:

The puppets themselves are true works of art! Each puppet is meticulously handcrafted, featuring elaborate costumes, detailed facial expressions, and articulated joints that allow them to move gracefully during performances.

Intriguing Puppet Characters:

Prepare to be introduced to a diverse cast of puppet characters, from legendary heroes and mythical creatures to comedic figures and historical personalities. These characters embody the essence of Taiwanese folklore and traditional stories.

Compelling Storytelling:

Puppetry performances are a unique form of storytelling. The puppeteers skillfully maneuver the puppets on a miniature stage, accompanied by traditional music and dramatic narration. The combination of movement, music, and storytelling creates a mesmerizing experience.

Fascinating Puppet Manipulation:

The art of puppet manipulation is awe-inspiring. Puppeteers expertly control the puppets' movements, using strings and rods with impressive dexterity. It's a delicate dance that requires precision and coordination.

Cultural Significance:

Traditional Taiwanese Puppetry plays an important role in preserving Taiwanese cultural heritage. It serves as a bridge between the past and the present, keeping ancient stories and traditions alive for future generations.

Revival and Modern Adaptations:

While rooted in tradition, puppetry has also seen modern adaptations, infusing contemporary themes and artistic techniques. This dynamic fusion ensures that puppetry continues to captivate audiences of all ages.

Cultural Festivals and Performances:

Throughout Taiwan, you'll find festivals and cultural events that feature Traditional Taiwanese Puppetry. Attending one of these performances is a delightful way to immerse yourself in the rich cultural tapestry of the island.

Conclusion:

There you have it—my insider's guide to Traditional Taiwanese Puppetry, an entrancing art form that weaves together history, craftsmanship, and captivating storytelling. Embrace the cultural heritage, appreciate the artistry, and let Traditional Taiwanese Puppetry transport you to a world of mythical legends and captivating narratives. Happy exploration, and may your encounter with puppetry leave you enchanted and inspired by the cultural treasures of Taiwan!

Celebrating Taipei's Festivals

Welcome to the vibrant world of celebrating Taipei's festivals, where the city comes alive with color, music, and cultural splendor. As an insider who has experienced the joyous festivities, immersed in the cultural traditions, and celebrated alongside the locals, I'm excited to share my personal insights with you. So, let's embark on a virtual journey through the diverse and exciting festivals that grace the streets of Taipei!

Lunar New Year Celebrations:

The Lunar New Year kicks off the festive season with a bang! Taipei transforms into a sea of red lanterns, vibrant parades, and lively dragon dances. Families come together to welcome the new year, exchange blessings, and enjoy sumptuous feasts that symbolize prosperity.

Lantern Festival Extravaganza:

The Lantern Festival is a sight to behold! Taipei illuminates with stunning lantern displays and artistic light installations. From traditional paper lanterns to modern LED creations, the city glows with artistic brilliance, creating a magical atmosphere.

Dragon Boat Festival Traditions:

The Dragon Boat Festival is all about action and excitement! Watch as teams race elaborately decorated dragon boats down the rivers, their rhythmic paddling accompanied by the beat of drums. It's a high-energy event that celebrates teamwork and camaraderie.

Taipei Jazz Festival Groove:

Calling all music lovers! The Taipei Jazz Festival sets the city swinging to the smooth sounds of jazz. World-class musicians take the stage, and parks and squares become impromptu jazz venues, creating a harmonious atmosphere.

Ghost Month and Zhongyuan Festival:

Ghost Month is a unique cultural experience in Taipei. During this time, locals pay homage to their ancestors and appease wandering spirits with elaborate ceremonies and performances. The Zhongyuan Festival, also known as the Hungry Ghost Festival, features captivating street operas and traditional performances.

Mid-Autumn Festival Moonlit Reverie:

The Mid-Autumn Festival is a time for family reunions and moonlit festivities. Lantern-lit gardens, mooncake feasts, and captivating folklore performances make this festival truly enchanting.

Double Ninth Festival's High Spirits:

The Double Ninth Festival is a celebration of spirit and vitality. People climb mountains to gain blessings and enjoy the picturesque views of Taipei's natural beauty.

Taipei Film Festival Showtime:

Film buffs, this one's for you! The Taipei Film Festival showcases a diverse selection of local and international films, with screenings, workshops, and discussions that cater to every cinematic taste.

Taipei Arts Festival Extravaganza:

Art takes center stage during the Taipei Arts Festival. This event presents a fusion of contemporary performances, theatrical shows, dance productions, and immersive art experiences that ignite the imagination.

Conclusion:

There you have it—my insider's guide to celebrating Taipei's festivals, a captivating kaleidoscope of cultural experiences. From the dazzling Lunar New Year to the melodious Taipei Jazz Festival, each celebration offers a unique insight into Taiwanese traditions and artistic expressions. Embrace the lively parades, immerse yourself in the cultural festivities, and let the spirit of Taipei's festivals ignite your passion for culture, music, and art. Happy celebration, and may your experience be filled with unforgettable moments of joy, camaraderie, and cultural wonder!

Indulge in Taiwanese Cuisine

Must-Try Taiwanese Street Food

Hey there, fellow foodie adventurer! Welcome to the tantalizing world of Taiwanese street food, where delectable delights await your taste buds at every corner. As an insider who has explored the bustling night markets, savored the mouthwatering treats, and embraced the local food culture, I'm excited to share my personal insights with you. So, let's embark on a virtual gastronomic journey through the must-try Taiwanese street food that will surely leave you craving for more!

Night Market Bliss:

Taiwanese street food is best experienced in the vibrant night markets that come alive after dusk. The tantalizing aroma of sizzling dishes and the lively atmosphere set the perfect stage for an unforgettable culinary adventure.

Stinky Tofu Sensation:

Don't be fooled by the name! Stinky Tofu is a beloved Taiwanese delicacy. The deep-fried tofu boasts a pungent aroma but offers a surprisingly delicious and crispy texture. Trust me, it's a must-try for any food explorer.

Oyster Omelette Delight:

The Oyster Omelette is a savory treat you'll find at every night market. It features plump oysters embedded in a luscious egg omelette, topped with a tangy and flavorful sauce that will leave your taste buds dancing.

Braised Pork Rice Perfection:

Sink your teeth into the succulent goodness of Braised Pork Rice, a classic Taiwanese comfort food. Tender, flavorful chunks of pork are served over steaming white rice, creating a soul-satisfying combination that locals adore.

Scallion Pancake Crisps:

Crispy on the outside and chewy on the inside, Scallion Pancakes are a street food favorite. These savory delights are often filled with chopped scallions, creating an aromatic and flavorful snack.

Bubble Tea Bliss:

You can't visit Taiwan without trying Bubble Tea, the beloved Taiwanese invention. Sip on a refreshing blend of tea, milk, and chewy tapioca pearls that come in various flavors. It's the perfect way to beat the heat!

Gua Bao Buns Galore:

Sink your teeth into Gua Bao, a delightful street food that features tender braised pork belly, pickled mustard greens, crushed peanuts, and fresh cilantro, all nestled in a soft steamed bun. One bite, and you'll be hooked!

Grilled Squid Spectacle:

Spot vendors grilling large squids on open flames, and you're in for a treat. The grilled squid is seasoned to perfection and offers a delightful combination of smoky and savory flavors.

Sweet Potato Ball Bliss:

Crispy on the outside and soft on the inside, Sweet Potato Balls are a sweet street food indulgence. These golden-fried treats are a favorite among locals and visitors alike.

Conclusion:

There you have it—my insider's guide to must-try Taiwanese street food, a culinary journey that unveils the flavorful heart of Taiwan's vibrant food scene. From the savory Oyster Omelette to the sweet Bubble Tea, each delicacy offers a unique and unforgettable taste of Taiwan's culinary heritage. Embrace the diverse flavors, immerse yourself in the bustling night markets, and let the must-try Taiwanese street food leave an indelible mark on your food-loving soul. Happy culinary exploration, and may your street food adventure be filled with mouthwatering delights and cherished memories!

Din Tai Fung

Welcome to the world of Din Tai Fung, a legendary culinary treasure hailing from Taiwan. As an insider who has indulged in the delectable delights, marveled at the artistry of their signature dishes, and relished the warm ambiance, I'm thrilled to share my personal insights with you. So, let's embark on a virtual gastronomic journey through the iconic Din Tai Fung, where dumplings and culinary excellence await!

A Global Phenomenon:

Din Tai Fung has garnered international fame for its exceptional culinary craftsmanship, particularly its mouthwatering dumplings. What began as a humble street stall in Taipei has now become a global phenomenon, with numerous branches gracing cities worldwide.

The Dumpling Maestros:

Din Tai Fung's mastery lies in its dumplings, meticulously handcrafted by skilled artisans. These delicate parcels of joy boast a perfectly thin skin, encasing a delicious filling that bursts with flavor in every bite.

Xiaolongbao Wonder:

Xiaolongbao, the crown jewel of Din Tai Fung, is a type of soup dumpling. These little parcels are filled with savory meat and a mouthwatering broth, making them a delightful explosion of taste and texture.

A Symphony of Flavors:

The menu at Din Tai Fung extends far beyond dumplings. From savory buns and noodles to delectable appetizers and desserts, each dish is thoughtfully prepared to create a symphony of flavors.

Freshness and Quality:

At Din Tai Fung, freshness and quality are paramount. Ingredients are carefully sourced to ensure each dish upholds the restaurant's high standards, delivering an unparalleled dining experience.

Elegant Simplicity:

The elegance of Din Tai Fung lies in its simplicity. Diners are presented with a menu that highlights the finest ingredients and culinary expertise, allowing the flavors to shine through without unnecessary adornments.

An Immersive Dining Experience:

Stepping into Din Tai Fung feels like entering a culinary sanctuary. The soothing ambiance, attentive service, and open kitchen where chefs craft each dumpling create an immersive and inviting dining experience.

Cultural Heritage:

Beyond the gastronomic wonders, Din Tai Fung embodies Taiwanese cultural heritage. The restaurant's commitment to quality, hospitality, and tradition pays homage to Taiwan's culinary legacy.

Dumpling Varieties:

Din Tai Fung offers an impressive range of dumpling varieties to suit diverse palates. Whether you're a fan of pork, chicken, shrimp, or vegetarian options, there's a dumpling to suit every taste.

Conclusion:

There you have it—my insider's guide to Din Tai Fung, a culinary haven that has won the hearts of food lovers worldwide. From the heavenly Xiaolongbao to the array of delightful dishes, each bite at Din Tai Fung is an exquisite experience. Embrace the artistry, savor the flavors, and let Din Tai Fung transport you to a realm of dumpling perfection and culinary delight. Happy dining, and may your experience at Din Tai Fung be filled with unforgettable moments of gastronomic bliss and cherished memories!

Night Market Delights

Welcome to the bustling world of Night Market Delights, where the streets of Taiwan come alive with a feast for the senses. As an insider who has wandered through the enchanting night markets, savored the mouthwatering treats, and embraced the lively atmosphere, I'm excited to share my personal insights with you. So, let's embark on a virtual gastronomic journey through the captivating world of Night Market Delights!

Night Market Culture:

Night markets are an integral part of Taiwanese culture. As the sun sets, these vibrant markets awaken, transforming the streets into a culinary wonderland. The mingling aromas, colorful stalls, and lively chatter create an atmosphere like no other.

Stroll and Savor:

When you step into a night market, take your time to stroll and savor the diverse offerings. Each stall promises a unique culinary experience that will tempt your taste buds and leave you craving for more.

Omnivore's Paradise:

Night markets cater to every palate, making them an omnivore's paradise. From savory street food to sweet delicacies, vegetarian delights to sizzling meats, there's something for everyone to enjoy.

Stinky Tofu Temptation:

Don't be deterred by the pungent aroma! Stinky Tofu is a must-try Taiwanese delicacy. The deep-fried tofu boasts a crispy exterior, while its soft and flavorful interior creates a unique and addictive culinary experience.

Bubble Tea Bliss:

A night market adventure wouldn't be complete without indulging in Bubble Tea. Sip on the refreshing blend of tea, milk, and chewy tapioca pearls as you explore the market's vibrant offerings.

Savory Oyster Omelette:

The Oyster Omelette is a tantalizing delight you'll find at almost every night market. The succulent oysters nestled in a fluffy egg omelette, drizzled with a tangy sauce, create a mouthwatering combination.

Stuffed Buns and Baozi:

Treat yourself to a variety of stuffed buns and baozi. These soft, fluffy buns are filled with a delectable assortment of savory or sweet fillings, making them a popular snack among locals.

Grilled Skewers Galore:

Follow the enticing aroma of grilled skewers as you weave through the night market. From succulent meats to mouthwatering vegetables, the grilled skewers offer a delightful explosion of flavors.

Taiwanese Pancake Pleasures:

Crispy on the outside and filled with flavorful ingredients, Taiwanese pancakes are a delightful treat. Whether you choose a savory or sweet filling, these pancakes are sure to satisfy your cravings.

Conclusion:

There you have it—my insider's guide to Night Market Delights, a culinary adventure that celebrates the heart and soul of Taiwan's vibrant street food culture. From the sizzling skewers to the sweet Bubble Tea, each delicacy offers a unique and unforgettable taste of the night market's charm. Embrace the lively atmosphere, savor the diverse flavors, and let Night Market Delights transport you to a world of culinary wonders and cherished memories. Happy exploration, and may your night market experience be filled with mouthwatering delights and unforgettable moments!

Bubble Tea Craze

Welcome to the fascinating world of the Bubble Tea Craze, a delightful and refreshing beverage phenomenon that has taken the globe by storm. As an insider who has savored countless cups of this beloved drink, explored its diverse flavors, and embraced the cultural phenomenon, I'm excited to share my personal insights with you. So, let's embark on a virtual journey through the enchanting world of Bubble Tea Craze!

Origins of Bubble Tea:

Bubble tea, also known as boba tea, originated in Taiwan in the 1980s. It was an innovative creation that combined traditional tea with the addition of chewy tapioca pearls, creating a unique and playful texture.

Diverse Flavors and Options:

The beauty of bubble tea lies in its diverse flavors and customizable options. From classic milk teas to fruity infusions and even cheese-topped variations, there's a bubble tea for every taste preference.

The Art of Tapioca Pearls:

The chewy tapioca pearls are a defining feature of bubble tea. These little spheres are cooked to perfection, adding a fun and delightful texture to each sip.

Customization Galore:

When ordering bubble tea, feel free to customize your drink to your heart's desire. Adjust the sugar level, ice, and toppings to create a personalized beverage that suits your taste perfectly.

Innovative Toppings:

Bubble tea shops often push the boundaries of creativity with their toppings. From colorful popping boba to aloe vera jelly and pudding, the options for unique toppings are endless.

Cheese-Topped Sensation:

One of the latest trends in bubble tea is the cheese-topped version, where a creamy cheese foam is added to the top of the drink. The combination of sweet and savory flavors creates a delightful taste sensation.

Bubble Tea Culture and Social Media:

Bubble tea culture has become more than just a drink; it's a social experience. People love to share their bubble tea adventures on social media, showcasing not just the beverage but also the aesthetic and fun of the entire experience.

Global Phenomenon:

What started as a local Taiwanese drink has now become a global phenomenon. Bubble tea shops have popped up in cities all over the world, enchanting people with their delightful beverages.

Innovations and Experiments:

The bubble tea craze continues to evolve, with constant innovations and experiments. You might come across unique flavor combinations or limited-edition creations that keep the excitement alive.

Conclusion:

There you have it—my insider's guide to the Bubble Tea Craze, a captivating journey through the world of this beloved beverage. From the origins in Taiwan to the global sensation it has become, bubble tea continues to enchant people of all ages. Embrace the diverse flavors, savor the chewy tapioca pearls, and let the Bubble Tea Craze add a touch of sweetness and delight to your day. Happy sipping, and may your bubble tea adventures be filled with endless moments of joy and cherished memories!

Michelin-Starred Dining

Welcome to the exclusive world of Michelin-starred dining, where culinary artistry and gastronomic excellence collide. As an insider who has experienced the sheer brilliance of Michelin-starred restaurants, tasted the impeccable creations of world-renowned chefs, and relished the exquisite flavors of each dish, I'm thrilled to share my personal insights with you. So, let's embark on a virtual culinary journey through the enchanting realm of Michelin-starred dining!

Coveted Michelin Stars:

Michelin stars are the culinary world's highest honor, awarded to exceptional restaurants for their outstanding quality and creativity. Each star signifies a level of excellence that elevates a dining experience to unparalleled heights.

Epicurean Delights:

At Michelin-starred restaurants, dining is more than just a meal; it's a symphony of flavors that tantalize the taste buds and delight the senses. Each dish is a masterpiece, carefully crafted with precision and passion.

Artistry on a Plate:

Prepare to be amazed by the artistry of each dish. Michelin-starred chefs are true culinary artists, combining exquisite presentation with complex flavors, creating plates that are almost too beautiful to eat.

Gourmet Menus and Degustation:

Michelin-starred restaurants often offer gourmet menus and degustation experiences. These multi-course journeys take diners on a culinary adventure, showcasing the chef's creativity and culinary prowess.

Elevating Local Ingredients:

One of the hallmarks of Michelin-starred dining is the use of locally sourced, fresh ingredients. Chefs often showcase the best of the region's produce, elevating traditional flavors to new heights.

Meticulous Attention to Detail:

Every aspect of a Michelin-starred dining experience is carefully curated. From the elegant table settings to the impeccable service, no detail is overlooked in creating a memorable and indulgent experience.

Culinary Innovation:

Michelin-starred chefs are pioneers of culinary innovation. They push the boundaries of gastronomy, infusing traditional recipes with modern techniques and unexpected ingredients.

A Memorable Affair:

Dining at a Michelin-starred restaurant is an unforgettable affair. It's an opportunity to savor not only exceptional dishes but also the passion and dedication of the chefs who pour their heart and soul into their craft.

Reservations and Planning:

Securing a reservation at a Michelin-starred restaurant is highly recommended, as these establishments tend to be in high demand. Planning ahead ensures that you can secure a coveted spot for your dining experience.

Conclusion:

There you have it—my insider's guide to Michelin-starred dining, an extraordinary journey into the realm of culinary excellence. From the epicurean delights to the artistry on the plate, each moment at a Michelin-starred restaurant is a celebration of gastronomic brilliance. Embrace the world-class flavors, savor the meticulous attention to detail, and let Michelin-starred dining transport you to a realm of culinary wonder and unforgettable memories. Happy dining, and may your gastronomic adventures be filled with endless moments of culinary bliss and cherished experiences!

Nature and Outdoor Escapes

Yangmingshan National Park

Welcome to the breathtaking beauty of Yangmingshan National Park, a serene escape nestled in the heart of Taiwan. As an insider who has explored the lush landscapes, marveled at the scenic wonders, and embraced the tranquility of this national park, I'm excited to share my personal insights with you. So, let's embark on a virtual journey through the enchanting world of Yangmingshan National Park!

Nature's Wonderland:

Yangmingshan National Park is a true paradise for nature lovers. The park's diverse landscapes boast a mesmerizing combination of rolling hills, hot springs, volcanic mountains, and vibrant floral displays that change with the seasons.

Breathtaking Scenic Beauty:

From the stunning vistas at the volcanic peaks to the calming waters of the lakes and streams, the scenic beauty of Yangmingshan is simply awe-inspiring. Prepare to be captivated by the harmony of nature's colors and textures.

Hot Springs Retreat:

Yangmingshan is renowned for its therapeutic hot springs. Immerse yourself in the soothing waters and let the warmth melt away your cares, creating a blissful experience of relaxation and rejuvenation.

Floral Symphony:

If you visit during the spring months, be prepared to witness a breathtaking floral symphony. The cherry blossoms, azaleas, and calla lilies create a vibrant tapestry that blankets the hills, turning the park into a floral wonderland.

Hiking Trails and Adventure:

For outdoor enthusiasts, Yangmingshan offers an array of hiking trails that cater to all skill levels. Whether you're an avid hiker seeking challenging treks or a leisurely stroller wanting to enjoy the scenery, there's a trail for you.

Hidden Gems and Waterfalls:

The national park is filled with hidden gems, including tranquil waterfalls tucked away in the lush forests. Explore the lesser-known spots for a peaceful encounter with nature.

Geothermal Wonderland:

Yangmingshan's volcanic terrain gives rise to geothermal wonders. You'll come across fumaroles and sulfur deposits, offering a glimpse into the park's unique geological features.

Picnic Perfect:

Pack a picnic basket and find a serene spot to enjoy a meal amidst nature's embrace. Whether it's by a tranquil pond or on a grassy hill, a picnic in Yangmingshan is an unforgettable experience.

Seasonal Delights:

Each season in Yangmingshan brings its own enchantment. From the colorful blooms of spring to the vibrant hues of autumn, every visit promises a unique and memorable experience.

Conclusion:

There you have it—my insider's guide to Yangmingshan National Park, a nature lover's haven that offers a harmonious blend of scenic beauty and tranquility. Embrace the breathtaking landscapes, soak in the healing hot springs, and let Yangmingshan's natural wonders transport you to a world of serenity and peace. Happy exploration, and may your journey through Yangmingshan be filled with unforgettable moments of nature's wonder and cherished memories!

Jiufen

Welcome to the enchanting world of Jiufen, a picturesque mountain town that seems to have stepped out of a fairytale. As an insider who has roamed its charming streets, uncovered hidden gems, and embraced the nostalgic ambiance, I'm excited to share my personal insights with you. So, let's embark on a virtual journey through the captivating allure of Jiufen!

Nostalgic Old Streets:

Jiufen's old streets are a gateway to the past, where traditional Taiwanese architecture and narrow alleys create an atmosphere of nostalgia. Prepare to be transported back in time as you stroll through the charming lanes lined with tea houses, souvenir shops, and street vendors.

Teahouse Haven:

Insider: Jiufen is renowned for its teahouses, offering a serene escape with breathtaking views of the surrounding mountains and ocean. Sip on a fragrant cup of tea while taking in the tranquil beauty of the landscape.

A-Mei Tea House Legacy:

Don't miss the A-Mei Tea House, an iconic establishment that inspired the famous Studio Ghibli film "Spirited Away." This teahouse is steeped in history and offers a glimpse into the town's cultural heritage.

Breathtaking Scenic Vistas:

The scenic vistas of Jiufen are truly mesmerizing. Whether you're perched on a hilltop overlooking the ocean or gazing at the town's labyrinth of rooftops, the views are simply breathtaking.

Local Delicacies and Street Food:

Jiufen is a food lover's paradise. Indulge in delectable local delicacies and street food as you explore the bustling markets. From savory taro balls to sweet pineapple cakes, your taste buds are in for a treat!

Gold Rush Heritage:

Jiufen has a fascinating history of a gold rush era, and remnants of this heritage can still be found. The Gold Museum is a must-visit to learn about the town's gold mining past.

Lantern-Lit Evenings:

As the sun sets, Jiufen transforms into a mesmerizing wonderland with lantern-lit evenings. The soft glow of lanterns adds a touch of magic to the already charming streets.

Hidden Stairways and Alleys:

Venture beyond the main streets, and you'll discover hidden stairways and alleys that lead to picturesque corners and secret viewpoints. Be prepared to uncover the town's hidden treasures.

Inspirational Art and Culture:

Jiufen has inspired numerous artists and writers with its captivating beauty. Many galleries and art installations reflect the town's influence on creativity and cultural expression.

Conclusion:

There you have it—my insider's guide to Jiufen, a magical mountain town brimming with nostalgia and charm. Embrace the teahouse havens, savor the local flavors, and let Jiufen's enchanting beauty captivate your heart. Happy exploration, and may your journey through Jiufen be filled with unforgettable moments of wonder and cherished memories!

Wulai

Welcome to the captivating world of Wulai, a hidden gem nestled in the mountains of Taiwan. As an insider who has explored the natural wonders, embraced the indigenous culture, and discovered the peaceful charm of this quaint town, I'm excited to share my personal insights with you. So, let's embark on a virtual journey through the enchanting allure of Wulai!

Indigenous Heritage:

Wulai is home to the Atayal indigenous tribe, and their rich cultural heritage is woven into every aspect of the town. From traditional crafts to colorful festivals, you'll get a glimpse of their fascinating way of life.

Wulai Old Street:

Stroll through Wulai Old Street, a bustling market where you can find authentic Atayal crafts, souvenirs, and delicious local snacks. The warm smiles of the locals and the lively atmosphere add to the charm of this place.

Wulai Waterfalls:

Prepare to be amazed by Wulai's stunning waterfalls. The Wulai Waterfall, in particular, is a majestic sight, cascading down the mountainside and surrounded by lush greenery. Take a relaxing walk along the trails to get up close and personal with nature's beauty.

Hot Springs Retreat:

Wulai is famous for its hot springs, and you won't want to miss the chance to soak in the healing waters. The soothing warmth of the springs is the perfect remedy for tired muscles and a wonderful way to unwind.

Wulai Cable Car:

Hop on the Wulai Cable Car for a thrilling ride that offers breathtaking aerial views of the valley below. The cable car takes you to the top of the mountain, where you can enjoy panoramic vistas of the surrounding landscape.

Traditional Atayal Cuisine:

Don't miss the opportunity to savor traditional Atayal cuisine. The local delicacies, often made with fresh and locally sourced ingredients, offer a unique and flavorful culinary experience.

Hiking and Nature Trails:

For outdoor enthusiasts, Wulai offers a network of hiking and nature trails that lead you through serene forests and past scenic viewpoints. It's the perfect way to immerse yourself in the natural beauty of the area.

Wulai Tram:

Take a ride on the Wulai Tram, a charming and eco-friendly mode of transportation that winds its way through the town and offers a leisurely way to explore the sights.

Preserving Indigenous Culture:

Wulai takes great pride in preserving and showcasing its indigenous culture. The cultural performances, art displays, and traditional events offer a glimpse into the heart of the Atayal community.

Conclusion:

There you have it—my insider's guide to Wulai, a picturesque mountain town that celebrates indigenous heritage and natural beauty. Embrace the warm hospitality, indulge in traditional delicacies, and let Wulai's serene charm captivate your soul. Happy exploration, and may your journey through Wulai be filled with unforgettable moments of cultural discovery and cherished memories!

Yehliu Geopark

Welcome to the captivating world of Yehliu Geopark, a geological wonderland situated along Taiwan's northern coast. As an insider who has explored the unique rock formations, marveled at the natural artistry, and embraced the coastal beauty, I'm excited to share my personal insights with you. So, let's embark on a virtual journey through the enchanting allure of Yehliu Geopark!

A Geological Masterpiece:

Yehliu Geopark is a geological masterpiece shaped by millions of years of natural forces. The park's unique rock formations, sculpted by wind and sea erosion, resemble a gallery of intriguing sculptures.

The Queen's Head:

One of the most iconic formations in Yehliu Geopark is the Queen's Head—a majestic rock resembling the profile of a queen wearing a crown.

This natural wonder draws visitors from far and wide to marvel at its likeness.

Fairy Shoe and Mushroom Rocks:

As you wander through the park, keep an eye out for the Fairy Shoe and Mushroom Rocks. These whimsical formations will spark your imagination and transport you to a fantastical world.

Coastal Beauty:

Yehliu Geopark's coastal setting offers breathtaking views of the turquoise sea and rocky shoreline. The sight of waves crashing against the unique rock formations creates a mesmerizing spectacle.

Nature's Artistry:

Each rock formation in Yehliu Geopark is a testament to nature's artistry. As you explore the park, you'll be awestruck by the intricate patterns and textures etched into the rocks over millennia.

Time and Tide Pools:

The tidal pools within the geopark provide a fascinating glimpse into marine life. During low tide, you can observe various marine creatures, colorful algae, and sea anemones thriving in these pools.

Geological Exhibitions:

Yehliu Geopark offers informative exhibitions that explain the geological processes behind the rock formations. The exhibits enhance your understanding of the park's scientific significance.

Nature's Healing:

Yehliu Geopark's serene ambiance and breathtaking vistas make it an ideal place for relaxation and contemplation. The sound of crashing waves and the coastal breeze provide a soothing environment to unwind.

Photographer's Paradise:

If you're a photography enthusiast, Yehliu Geopark will be a paradise of picture-perfect moments. Capture the beauty of the rock formations, the dramatic coastline, and the interplay of light and shadows.

Conclusion:

There you have it—my insider's guide to Yehliu Geopark, a geological wonderland that showcases the artistry of nature. Embrace the unique rock formations, savor the coastal beauty, and let Yehliu Geopark's natural wonders leave an indelible mark on your heart. Happy exploration, and may your journey through Yehliu Geopark be filled with unforgettable moments of awe and cherished memories!

Danshui Fisherman's Wharf

Welcome to the delightful world of Danshui Fisherman's Wharf, a charming waterfront destination in Taiwan. As an insider who has wandered through the bustling wharf, savored the freshest seafood, and embraced the scenic beauty, I'm thrilled to share my personal insights with you. So, let's embark on a virtual journey through the enchanting allure of Danshui Fisherman's Wharf!

Coastal Serenity:

Danshui Fisherman's Wharf is a serene escape along the coastline of northern Taiwan. The tranquil waters and scenic views create a peaceful ambiance, making it a perfect spot to unwind and soak in the maritime charm.

Bustling Wharf Culture:

The wharf is a hub of activity, brimming with energy and life. As you walk along the wooden boardwalks, you'll encounter bustling seafood restaurants, quirky boutiques, and picturesque spots for a leisurely stroll.

Sunset Delights:

Danshui Fisherman's Wharf is renowned for its breathtaking sunsets. The sky transforms into a canvas of vibrant colors, casting a warm glow over the waterfront, making it an idyllic setting for romantic moments.

Lover's Bridge:

One of the highlights of the wharf is the Lover's Bridge, an arched footbridge that stretches gracefully over the river. At night, it transforms into a twinkling spectacle of lights, creating a dreamy atmosphere.

Fresh Seafood Feast:

Prepare your taste buds for a delectable seafood feast! The wharf's restaurants offer an array of freshly caught seafood dishes that are sure to satisfy any seafood lover's cravings.

Fishing and Sailing Experiences:

You're feeling adventurous, consider joining a fishing or sailing experience. Catching fish with the locals or setting sail along the coast allows you to immerse yourself in the region's fishing heritage.

Danhai Light Rail:

The Danhai Light Rail is a convenient way to explore the area. Hop on the charming tram and take in the coastal scenery as it shuttles you between various attractions.

Riverside Promenade:

The riverside promenade offers a refreshing escape from the city's hustle and bustle. Take a leisurely walk or rent a bicycle to enjoy the river breeze and picturesque views.

Cultural Events and Festivals:

Keep an eye out for cultural events and festivals that take place at the wharf. From lively concerts to vibrant celebrations, these events add an extra layer of charm to your visit.

Conclusion:

There you have it—my insider's guide to Danshui Fisherman's Wharf, a charming waterfront destination that combines coastal serenity with bustling wharf culture. Embrace the stunning sunsets, savor the freshest seafood, and let Danshui Fisherman's Wharf's maritime allure leave a lasting impression. Happy exploration, and may your journey through the wharf be filled with unforgettable moments of tranquility and cherished memories!

Retail Therapy and Shopping

Xinyi District

Welcome to Xinyi District, Taipei's bustling shopping hub, where retail therapy takes on a whole new meaning. Here, the vibrant streets and modern architecture blend seamlessly, offering an electrifying experience that shopaholics and fashion enthusiasts crave. Let's embark on a journey through the heart of Xinyi, unveiling its hidden gems and ultimate shopping delights, just like an insider.

The Iconic Taipei 101

As you step into Xinyi District, the first thing that catches your eye is the iconic Taipei 101. This architectural marvel stands tall and proud, symbolizing the modernity of Taipei. Take a moment to admire its beauty, especially during the evening when the city lights illuminate the surrounding area, creating a mesmerizing sight.

Luxury Galore at Taipei 101 Mall

Prepare yourself for an unforgettable shopping experience at the Taipei 101 Mall. Step inside, and you'll find a stunning array of high-end boutiques and international luxury brands. From designer fashion to exquisite jewelry, every corner exudes opulence and exclusivity. It's here that retail therapy reaches new heights, and shopaholics revel in the splendor of their surroundings.

Xinyi Shopping Wonderland at ATT 4 FUN

Venture a little further and you'll stumble upon the vibrant and lively ATT 4 FUN. This multi-story shopping complex is a paradise for the young and trendy. Fashion-forward locals and visitors alike flock to the countless boutiques offering the latest clothing trends, quirky accessories, and unique gadgets. ATT 4 FUN is the go-to destination for those seeking fashion statements that express their individuality.

Discover Eslite Spectrum

Bookworms and culture enthusiasts will find their haven at Eslite Spectrum, a multi-story cultural center and bookstore. Lose yourself in the vast collection of books covering every genre imaginable. The serene ambiance and soft jazz music make it an ideal spot to unwind while flipping through pages. Eslite Spectrum also features a fantastic selection of art and design products, making it a treasure trove for creative minds.

Revitalize at Songshan Cultural and Creative Park

Escape the hustle and bustle of shopping and immerse yourself in creativity at the Songshan

Cultural and Creative Park. This transformed tobacco factory now serves as a hub for artistic exhibitions, craft fairs, and creative workshops. It's the perfect place to discover unique artisanal creations and get inspired by the rich Taiwanese culture.

The Xinyi Shopping Streets

Wander through the lively Xinyi shopping streets, where an eclectic mix of shops, street vendors, and local boutiques offer an array of goods. From trendy fashion to quirky souvenirs, you'll find something to suit your taste and budget. Bargaining is common here, so unleash your negotiation skills to snag the best deals.

Culinary Delights at Tonghua Night Market

Retail therapy works up an appetite, and there's no better place to satiate your cravings than the Tonghua Night Market. This bustling market is a foodie's paradise, offering a mouthwatering selection of Taiwanese delicacies and international cuisine. Sample local favorites like stinky tofu, oyster omelets, and bubble tea as you savor the vibrant atmosphere of this food haven.

A Night of Glitz and Glamour at Neo19

As the sun sets, Xinyi District transforms into a glamorous nightlife destination. Head to Neo19, a stylish entertainment complex that houses top-notch restaurants, trendy bars, and upscale clubs. Party-goers and night owls can dance the night away, rubbing shoulders with Taipei's fashion-forward elite.

Xinyi District is a retail therapy and shopping paradise where modernity and tradition collide, leaving visitors in awe of its energy and diversity. From luxury shopping to cultural exploration and mouthwatering culinary adventures, Xinyi offers a holistic experience that will leave an indelible mark on your heart and fashion-forward soul. Embrace the magic of Xinyi, and let retail therapy take you on an unforgettable journey through Taipei's most vibrant district.

Shilin Night Market

Welcome to Shilin Night Market, Taipei's legendary haven for retail therapy and shopping extravaganza. As an insider, I'll be your guide to unlock the secrets of this bustling nocturnal marketplace where sensory delights and vibrant energy combine to create an unforgettable experience. Get ready to immerse yourself in the captivating world of Shilin Night Market.

A Night Market Alight with Energy

As the sun sets, Shilin Night Market comes alive with a symphony of colors and sounds. Neon lights illuminate the bustling streets, beckoning you to enter a world of endless shopping possibilities. The air is filled with the aroma of sizzling street food, enticing you to indulge in Taiwan's culinary delights before you embark on your retail adventure.

Hidden Treasures in the Labyrinth of Stalls

Step into the labyrinth of stalls that make up Shilin Night Market, and you'll be transported to a treasure trove of unique finds. Each stall presents an array of products, from trendy fashion apparel to quirky accessories and artisanal crafts. As you weave through the maze, keep an eye out for hidden gems, one-of-a-kind items that reflect the ingenuity of local vendors.

Fashion Frenzy at Shilin Underground Market

Descend into the underground wonderland known as Shilin Underground Market. Here, you'll be captivated by the latest fashion trends and affordable clothing options. From streetwear to elegant dresses, the choices seem endless, catering to fashionistas with diverse styles and tastes. Prepare to shop till you drop as you discover fantastic deals on stylish apparel.

Unleashing Your Inner Foodie

Retail therapy at Shilin Night Market isn't limited to fashion and crafts; it's a gastronomic adventure too. Sample an assortment of mouthwatering Taiwanese snacks that fill the air with irresistible aromas. Sink your teeth into the iconic stinky tofu, crispy salt and pepper chicken, and the famous Taiwanese sausage. Let your taste buds dance with delight as you try unique delicacies like oyster omelets and bubble tea.

Bargaining Like a Pro

As an insider, I'll let you in on a little secret: bargaining is an art form at Shilin Night Market. Engage in friendly banter with the vendors, showcasing your haggling skills to score the best deals. Remember, a smile and a playful spirit go a long way in making your shopping experience even more enjoyable.

Embracing the Night Market Vibe

Shilin Night Market is more than just a shopping destination; it's an experience that embraces the essence of Taiwanese culture. Engage in lively conversations with locals and fellow shoppers, immersing yourself in the warm and welcoming atmosphere. Let the vibrant energy of the night market envelop you as you explore its nooks and crannies.

Unearth Traditional Arts and Crafts

For those seeking authentic Taiwanese crafts, the Shilin Night Market won't disappoint. Discover stalls adorned with beautifully crafted handmade goods, from delicate ceramics to intricate calligraphy. These traditional art pieces make for meaningful souvenirs and cherished gifts.

Embracing the Night

As the night deepens, the allure of Shilin Night Market intensifies. The crowds swell, and the atmosphere becomes even more vibrant. Engage in a game of skill at one of the many carnival-style games or witness impressive street performances by local artists. The night is alive with excitement and surprises, making it an unforgettable experience.

Shilin Night Market is a captivating amalgamation of retail therapy, culinary delights, and cultural immersion. As an insider, I assure you that this bustling marketplace will leave an indelible mark on your heart and create cherished memories of Taipei's vibrant spirit. So, slip into your comfortable shoes, embrace the night market vibe, and embark on a retail journey that promises to be unlike any other. Happy shopping!8.3 Underground Malls

Underground Malls

Welcome to the hidden realm of underground malls, a shopaholic's paradise nestled beneath the bustling streets of modern cities. As an insider, I will take you on a captivating journey through these subterranean shopping wonderlands, where retail therapy takes on a whole new dimension. Prepare to be enchanted by the vibrant atmosphere and exquisite finds that await you in the depths below.

The Subtle Entrance

As you step into the discreet entrance of the underground mall, the bustling city noise starts to fade away, replaced by a sense of anticipation. The cool, dimly lit corridor beckons you to leave the world above and delve into a secret retail haven. Excitement builds as you descend deeper, wondering what hidden treasures await your discovery.

Sublime Architecture and Artistry

Once inside the underground mall, you'll be amazed by the architectural marvels that surround you. A harmonious blend of modern design and artistic touches creates an ambiance that is both inviting and awe-inspiring. Intricate sculptures, captivating murals, and innovative lighting installations add a touch of elegance to the shopping experience, turning every corner into a visual delight.

Retail Haven for Fashionistas

Prepare to indulge in a fashion paradise as you enter the stylish boutiques that line the corridors. The underground mall boasts an impressive collection of trendy clothing, from haute couture to casual streetwear. Pamper yourself with a myriad of options that cater to every style and budget, making it a haven for fashion-forward individuals seeking that perfect ensemble.

Curating Your Personal Style

What sets underground malls apart is their focus on personalized shopping experiences. Knowledgeable and attentive shop assistants take the time to understand your preferences, guiding you through the vast collection of clothing, accessories, and footwear. Their expertise helps you curate a unique style that perfectly complements your personality, making you feel like a fashion icon.

Unearth Artisanal Gems

Embrace the joy of discovering artisanal treasures hidden within the labyrinthine passageways. Art galleries and craft stores showcase handcrafted jewelry, home decor, and artistic masterpieces that are a celebration of creativity and craftsmanship. Each piece tells a story, making it a cherished keepsake or a thoughtful gift for loved ones.

Savoring Gastronomic Delights

A sensory feast awaits you as you encounter delightful eateries and cozy cafes scattered throughout the underground mall. Take a break from shopping and treat yourself to gourmet delights that range from international cuisine to local specialties. Sip on expertly brewed coffee, savor aromatic pastries, or indulge in a tantalizing fusion of flavors that will leave your taste buds craving for more.

Unexpected Entertainment

As you continue your exploration, be prepared to encounter captivating performances and pop-up events. Talented musicians, dancers, and street artists add a touch of entertainment to your shopping experience. Pause for a while and become an audience to their talents, immersing yourself in the vibrant energy that permeates the underground mall.

The Joy of Surprise Finds

Amidst the well-known brands, be open to serendipitous discoveries in the lesser-known stores. You might stumble upon unique pieces that express your individuality, transforming them into cherished mementos of your underground shopping adventure.

Underground malls offer an unparalleled shopping experience that seamlessly blends creativity, style, and culture. As an insider, I can assure you that this hidden world of retail therapy will leave you with fond memories and a renewed appreciation for the art of shopping. So, don your most comfortable shoes, let curiosity be your guide, and immerse yourself in the enchanting realm of underground malls—a place where retail therapy takes on a magical and unforgettable form. Happy shopping!

Yongkang Street

Welcome to Yongkang Street, Taipei's charming shopping district where retail therapy takes on a whole new meaning. As an insider, I am thrilled to be your guide through this delightful haven of boutiques, cafes, and artisanal shops. Get ready to immerse yourself in the vibrant atmosphere and discover the hidden treasures that await you on this enchanting street.

The Quaint Facades

As you set foot on Yongkang Street, the first thing that captures your attention is the row of charming, traditional facades lining both sides of the street. These quaint buildings are adorned with vibrant signage, creating a visual feast that harks back to Taipei's rich heritage. The warm earthy colors and wooden accents exude a welcoming ambiance, drawing you into a world of retail exploration.

Boutiques and Local Shops

Yongkang Street is a haven for boutique lovers, where fashion enthusiasts can indulge in a curated collection of stylish clothing, accessories, and footwear. The local shops here take pride in offering unique designs that showcase Taiwan's fashion ingenuity. From elegant dresses to quirky accessories, each store exudes a distinct personality, inviting you to explore and find pieces that resonate with your style.

Personalized Service

One of the many charms of Yongkang Street is the personalized service provided by the shop owners. With a warm smile and genuine enthusiasm, they cater to your preferences and needs, creating a shopping experience that feels like visiting old friends. Whether you seek fashion advice or want to learn about the stories behind the products, these insiders are more than willing to share their knowledge.

Delightful Artisanal Crafts

Yongkang Street is a treasure trove of artisanal crafts and locally made products. Explore the intimate shops tucked away from the main street, and you'll discover exquisite ceramics, handcrafted leather goods, and intricate jewelry pieces. Each item is a testament to the craftsmanship and dedication of local artisans, making them unique and meaningful keepsakes.

Culinary Adventures

Retail therapy isn't just about shopping for fashion; it's also about indulging your taste buds. Yongkang Street boasts an array of charming cafes, teahouses, and bakeries that beckon you to savor their delectable offerings. Whether you're craving a freshly brewed cup of Taiwanese tea or a delicate pastry, the street's culinary scene has something to delight every palate.

Embracing Cultural Vibes

Beyond the shops and cafes, Yongkang Street is steeped in cultural vibes that add to its allure. Art galleries and bookstores provide an insight into Taiwan's creative scene, allowing you to connect with the local arts and literary community. Embrace the intellectual energy of the street as you immerse yourself in thought-provoking artworks and fascinating reads.

Discovering Hidden Courtyards

As you wander deeper into Yongkang Street, you might stumble upon hidden courtyards and charming alleys that offer a respite from the bustling crowd. These peaceful retreats, adorned with potted plants and artistic decor, make for a serene setting to take a moment and absorb the essence of the street's unique charm.

The Timeless Appeal

Yongkang Street strikes a perfect balance between tradition and modernity, making it a timeless destination for retail therapy. The fusion of old-world charm and contemporary creativity creates an experience that leaves a lasting impression. From the vintage-inspired boutiques to the cutting-edge designs, every corner of Yongkang Street is an expression of Taipei's vibrant spirit.

Yongkang Street is a hidden gem in Taipei, waiting to be explored by those seeking an authentic and enriching retail therapy experience. As an insider, I assure you that this charming street will not only satiate your shopping desires but also leave you with cherished memories and a deeper connection to Taiwan's culture and creativity. So, put on your walking shoes, embrace the spirit of discovery, and let Yongkang Street enchant you with its retail wonders. Happy shopping!

Family Fun in Taipei

Taipei Children's Amusement Park

Step into a world of wonder and laughter at Taipei Children's Amusement Park, where dreams come alive, and imaginations take flight. As an insider, I am thrilled to be your guide through this enchanting playground, where the joy of childhood knows no bounds. Join me as we embark on a journey through this whimsical wonderland and experience the magic firsthand.

A Colorful Entrance

As you approach the entrance of Taipei Children's Amusement Park, the bright and cheerful colors instantly captivate your attention. The gate stands tall, adorned with playful characters and whimsical designs, inviting you to leave the cares of the world behind and step into a realm of pure delight.

Glimpses of Wonderland

Upon entering, you'll catch glimpses of thrilling rides soaring into the sky and cheerful music filling the air. Laughter and excited chatter from children and parents alike create an infectious buzz of anticipation. It's a place where every corner is designed to spark joy and ignite the imagination.

The Carousel of Dreams

The iconic carousel stands at the heart of the amusement park, its intricately painted horses beckoning you to hop on and relive the charm of a bygone era. As the carousel starts to spin, you'll be transported to a simpler time, where the joy of riding a carousel transcends age, and a smile lights up the faces of riders young and old.

Adventure Awaits at the Roller Coasters

For the thrill-seekers, the amusement park offers exhilarating roller coasters that twist and turn, sending you on a heart-pounding adventure. Feel the rush of adrenaline as the wind whizzes past your face, and your heart races with excitement. The roller coasters are not just rides; they are thrilling journeys of courage and bravery.

Whimsical Fantasy Lands

Immerse yourself in themed fantasy lands that seem to have leaped straight out of storybooks. Explore magical kingdoms with castles and mythical creatures, where the young at heart can let their imagination run wild. Whether it's sailing with pirates or flying with fairies, these lands transport you to extraordinary worlds where anything is possible.

Laughter and Joy at the Playgrounds

The amusement park boasts well-designed playgrounds that promise endless fun for children of all ages. Slides, swings, climbing frames, and interactive play areas provide the perfect setting for kids to burn off their energy and forge lasting friendships. Parents watch with delight as their little ones experience the sheer joy of unbridled play.

Splashes of Joy in the Water Park

Cool off from the summer heat in the water park, where splashes of joy await. Colorful water slides, splash pads, and lazy rivers offer refreshing entertainment for both children and adults. The sound of laughter mingles with the sound of flowing water, creating a harmonious symphony of delight.

A Moment of Wonder in the Ferris Wheel

Before bidding adieu to the amusement park, take a moment to ride the Ferris wheel and savor the breathtaking panoramic views of Taipei. As the Ferris wheel gently ascends, you'll be treated to a bird's-eye view of the magical wonderland you've just explored. It's a moment to reflect on the memories created and the joy shared.

Taipei Children's Amusement Park is a world of enchantment and joy, where the happiness of children and families is at the core of every experience. As an insider, I can assure you that this whimsical wonderland will leave you with cherished memories and a heart filled with the magic of childhood. So, come and embrace the wonder, laughter, and pure delight that awaits you at Taipei Children's Amusement Park. Happy exploring!

Taipei Zoo

Welcome to Taipei Zoo, a captivating world where wildlife thrives amidst lush greenery, and the wonders of nature come alive. As an insider, I am delighted to be your guide through this extraordinary sanctuary, where animals and visitors share an unforgettable connection. Join me on this immersive adventure, and let's explore the hidden gems and heartwarming encounters that await you at Taipei Zoo.

The Gateway to Wildlife

As you step through the entrance of Taipei Zoo, the gentle rustling of leaves and the distant sounds of animal calls greet your ears. The aroma of nature envelops you, setting the stage for a journey into the wild. Tall trees and meandering pathways invite you to embark on a sensory-filled experience, leaving the bustling city behind for a while.

Encounters with Majestic Creatures

The zoo houses a diverse collection of animal habitats, each carefully designed to mimic the creatures' natural environment. Wander through lush rainforests to witness playful gibbons swinging from branch to branch, or catch a glimpse of majestic elephants cooling off in their spacious enclosure. These up-close encounters with animals are awe-inspiring, and they offer a sense of wonder and appreciation for the animal kingdom.

Connecting with Conservation

Taipei Zoo is not merely a place for entertainment; it is a hub for education and conservation. Numerous exhibits provide insightful information about endangered species and the importance of preserving their habitats. Engaging educational programs and interactive displays inspire visitors to become stewards of the environment, promoting a sense of responsibility towards the Earth's diverse wildlife.

Birdsong Serenade

As you stroll through the aviaries, a symphony of melodious bird songs fills the air. Taipei Zoo is home to a wide array of bird species, showcasing their vibrant colors and unique calls. Delight in watching graceful flamingos wade through serene ponds and vibrant parrots flaunt their stunning plumage. The aviaries offer a moment of tranquility, a perfect escape from the hustle and bustle of city life.

Playful Pals at the Children's Zoo

The Children's Zoo is a favorite among young visitors, where farm animals and small mammals welcome playful interactions. Feed friendly goats, pet fluffy rabbits, and watch curious meerkats scurry about. The laughter of children and the excitement of learning create an enchanting atmosphere, leaving a lasting impression on little adventurers.

Journey through the Aquarium

Escape the tropical heat and venture into the mesmerizing world of the aquarium. The underwater realm comes alive as you encounter a fascinating array of marine life. From graceful sea turtles gliding through the water to vibrant coral reefs teeming with life, the aquarium offers a window into the captivating mysteries of the ocean.

Captivating Panda Encounter

A highlight of Taipei Zoo is the Giant Panda House, where you can observe the adorable giant pandas up close. Watching these gentle giants munch on bamboo and playfully interact with each other evokes a sense of joy and awe. The pandas' charm and charisma make them instant crowd-pleasers, and capturing a glimpse of these rare creatures leaves visitors with unforgettable memories.

Soaring Heights: Maokong Gondola

To end your zoo adventure on a high note, take a scenic ride on the Maokong Gondola adjacent to the zoo. As the gondola ascends over the lush hills, breathtaking views of Taipei city and the surrounding mountains unfold before your eyes. It's a moment of serenity and contemplation, cherishing the beauty of nature's wonders.

Taipei Zoo is more than just a place to observe animals; it's a sanctuary of inspiration, education, and connection with the natural world. As an insider, I can assure you that this adventure into the wild will leave you with a renewed appreciation for wildlife and a profound sense of wonder. So, embrace the magic of Taipei Zoo, and let the captivating stories of its inhabitants weave their way into your heart. Happy exploring!

Taipei Water Park

Welcome to Taipei Water Park, where the heat of summer meets the cool thrill of aquatic wonderland. As an insider, I am thrilled to be your guide on this exhilarating journey through a world of water slides, splash zones, and endless fun. Join me as we dive into the heart of Taipei Water Park and uncover the splashes of joy that await both the young and the young at heart.

An Oasis of Aquatic Delights

As you enter Taipei Water Park, the sound of laughter and splashing water fills the air, creating an atmosphere of pure excitement. The vibrant colors of water slides and playful structures invite you to leave your worries behind and immerse yourself in a world of aquatic delights. It's a paradise where the promise of refreshing fun awaits at every turn.

Thrills at Water Slide Wonderland

The heart of Taipei Water Park lies in its water slide wonderland. From towering water slides that make your heart race to twisting tunnels that fill you with adrenaline, the array of slides caters to all levels of thrill-seekers. As you slide down, the rush of the water and the laughter of fellow adventurers create a symphony of joy.

The Lazy River Retreat

For those seeking a more leisurely experience, the lazy river beckons with its gentle currents and relaxed pace. Hop on a colorful float and let the river carry you along, passing lush greenery and enchanting water features. It's a moment of blissful serenity, where worries are washed away, and time seems to slow down.

Water Playgrounds for Little Adventurers

Taipei Water Park is a haven for young explorers, featuring water playgrounds designed for endless fun and boundless imagination. Watch as children giggle under water sprays, climb play structures, and splash in kiddie pools. The water park's safe and interactive environment nurtures a sense of wonder and joy in the little ones, leaving parents beaming with pride.

Aqua Dance Party

The excitement doesn't stop when the sun goes down. During special events, Taipei Water Park transforms into an aqua dance party extravaganza. Neon lights illuminate the water, and music fills the air as visitors dance and splash under the night sky. It's a magical experience that infuses the park with an electrifying energy.

Poolside Treats and Refreshments

Amidst the water adventures, recharge at the poolside food stalls and cafes. Savor refreshing ice creams, tropical fruit juices, and savory snacks that fuel your energy for more water park thrills. The vibrant atmosphere of the dining areas adds to the overall enjoyment, as you savor delicious treats under the shade of colorful umbrellas.

Embracing the Water Park Vibes

Beyond the attractions, Taipei Water Park's lively atmosphere is a reflection of the joy and camaraderie among visitors. Bond with new friends over shared excitement on water slides, exchange laughter in the splash zones, and enjoy water fights that leave everyone drenched but elated. It's a place where connections are made and memories are created.

The Last Splash of the Day

As the day draws to a close, take one last exhilarating ride down your favorite water slide. The adrenaline rush and the cool water embrace leave you with a sense of euphoria, a perfect ending to an unforgettable day at Taipei Water Park. As you bid farewell, you carry the echoes of laughter and the memories of watery adventures, knowing that you've experienced the heart and soul of this aquatic wonderland.

Taipei Water Park is a celebration of fun, joy, and shared experiences. As an insider, I assure you that this journey into aquatic paradise will leave you with cherished memories and a longing to return. So, come, dive in, and let Taipei Water Park immerse you in a world of splashes and smiles. Happy splashing!

Taipei 101 Observatory

Welcome to Taipei 101 Observatory, an iconic landmark that reaches for the skies and offers an unparalleled experience that defies gravity. As an insider, I am thrilled to be your guide on this breathtaking journey to the top, where the cityscape unfolds beneath you, and the world takes on a new perspective. Join me as we ascend to the heights of Taipei 101, discovering the wonders that await at this majestic observatory.

A Grand Entrance

As you enter the Taipei 101 building, the sense of grandeur is palpable. The elegant interiors and sleek design reflect the city's modernity, while the anticipation of the observatory adventure ahead fills the air. The journey to the top begins, and you find yourself in awe of the engineering marvel that stands before you.

The Enchanting Lift Ride

The high-speed elevators that transport visitors to the observatory are nothing short of extraordinary. As you step into the lift, the doors close, and the ascent begins. The elevator accelerates at an impressive speed, whisking you up to the 89th floor in a matter of seconds. The display inside the elevator shows the floors passing by like a time-lapse, leaving you with a thrilling feeling of exhilaration.

Panoramic Views at Cloud Nine

The moment the elevator doors open at Cloud Nine, you are greeted with a jaw-dropping panorama of Taipei's cityscape. The observatory's expansive windows offer unobstructed 360-degree views, allowing you to witness the urban sprawl and natural beauty in all its glory. The city's iconic landmarks, bustling streets, and verdant mountains paint a vivid picture of Taipei's unique blend of modernity and nature.

Thrills at the Outdoor Sky Deck

Stepping out onto the outdoor Sky Deck takes the experience to a whole new level. The rush of the wind against your face and the unimpeded views of Taipei's skyline create an adrenaline-pumping moment that leaves you breathless. With the city unfolding below you like a breathtaking tapestry, the Sky Deck is a surreal vantage point that ignites your sense of adventure.

Awe-Inspiring Taipei 101 Damper

At the heart of the observatory, you'll discover the remarkable Taipei 101 damper. This engineering marvel is both functional and fascinating, designed to stabilize the tower during typhoons and earthquakes. It's a testament to human ingenuity and innovation, reminding you of the technical prowess that makes Taipei 101 an architectural wonder.

A Moment of Zen at the Indoor Observatory

After the excitement of the Sky Deck, head to the indoor observatory to experience a moment of tranquility. The calming atmosphere and soft lighting create a soothing ambiance, allowing you to reflect on the beauty of the cityscape and appreciate the intricacies of Taipei's skyline.

A Taste of Elegance at the Exclusive Restaurant

For those seeking a culinary delight at Taipei 101, the exclusive restaurant on the 85th floor promises an unforgettable dining experience. Indulge in delectable international cuisine while savoring panoramic views of Taipei's vibrant city lights—a perfect way to conclude your observatory adventure with a touch of sophistication.

The Unforgettable Descent

As your time at the Taipei 101 Observatory comes to an end, take one last look at the city below before stepping back into the elevator for the descent. The memories of this mesmerizing journey will stay with you forever, reminding you of the heights you reached and the beauty you witnessed from the top of Taipei's magnificent skyline.

Taipei 101 Observatory is a testament to Taipei's ambition, innovation, and spirit. As an insider, I assure you that this captivating journey to the top will leave you with cherished memories and a newfound appreciation for the city's captivating beauty. So, come, embrace the heights, and let Taipei 101 Observatory take you on an unforgettable adventure above the clouds. Happy soaring!

Day Trips and Beyond

Jiufen and Shifen

Welcome to a day of exploration and wonder as we embark on captivating day trips to Jiufen and Shifen, two enchanting destinations that beckon with their timeless beauty and cultural allure. As an insider, I am thrilled to be your guide on this immersive journey, where the charm of old-world streets and the tranquility of nature blend harmoniously. Join me as we uncover the hidden treasures of these idyllic towns and create cherished memories that will last a lifetime.

Jiufen: A Journey through Time

Our adventure begins in Jiufen, a picturesque town that transports you to a bygone era of ancient streets and rich heritage. The narrow alleys wind through quaint tea houses, souvenir shops, and traditional red lanterns, offering a glimpse of traditional Taiwanese life. Stroll along the cobbled pathways, and you'll feel as though you've stepped into a living painting.

Tea House Delights

In Jiufen, immersing yourself in the local tea culture is a must. Step into one of the charming tea houses with wooden facades and tea-scented air. Savor a cup of freshly brewed oolong tea while gazing out at the panoramic views of the mountains and sea. The soothing ambience and scenic vistas create a moment of serenity and relaxation.

Lantern-Lit Charm

As the sun begins to set, Jiufen transforms into a magical wonderland with lantern-lit charm. The lanterns hanging gracefully overhead cast a warm glow on the streets, adding to the town's nostalgic ambiance. It's the perfect time to explore Jiufen Old Street and sample delectable snacks like fish balls, taro cakes, and steamed buns from the bustling food stalls.

Shifen: A Riverside Retreat

Next, we venture to Shifen, a tranquil village nestled alongside the Tamsui River. The sound of flowing water and the picturesque riverside promenade create an atmosphere of serenity. Take a leisurely stroll along the riverbanks, and you'll encounter the iconic Shifen Old Street, where red lanterns dangle from the sky, and souvenir shops beckon with their unique wares.

Sky Lantern Wishes

One of the highlights of Shifen is the opportunity to release a sky lantern into the sky, carrying your wishes and dreams with it. Choose a colorful lantern, write your heartfelt wishes on it, and watch as it soars high into the heavens. This timeless tradition is an experience that fills you with a sense of hope and unity with fellow dreamers.

Shifen Waterfall: Nature's Masterpiece

For a touch of nature's wonders, venture to Shifen Waterfall, Taiwan's most scenic waterfall. The powerful cascade plunges into a serene pool, surrounded by lush greenery. Stand on the observation deck, and you'll feel the cool mist gently kiss your skin as you marvel at the majestic beauty of this natural masterpiece.

A Taste of Local Delicacies

As our day trip nears its end, treat your taste buds to a feast of local delicacies. From savory oyster omelets to sweet taro balls, Shifen offers an array of delectable treats that showcase the region's culinary heritage. Savor each bite and let the flavors of the town leave a lasting impression.

Embracing the Unforgettable Memories

As the sun sets on our day trips to Jiufen and Shifen, you carry with you the enchanting memories of ancient streets, river views, and lantern-lit charm. These hidden treasures have left an indelible mark on your heart, and the allure of Jiufen and Shifen beckons you to return and explore more of their timeless beauty.

Jiufen and Shifen are a testament to Taiwan's rich heritage and natural splendor. As an insider, I assure you that this day trip will awaken your senses, ignite your sense of wonder, and leave you with a profound appreciation for the hidden gems of these idyllic towns. So, come, immerse yourself in the timeless charm, and let Jiufen and Shifen take you on an unforgettable journey of exploration and delight. Happy adventures!

Tamsuis

Embark on a day of tranquility and exploration as we delve into the hidden wonders of Tamsuis, a picturesque destination on the outskirts of Taipei. As an insider, I am thrilled to be your guide on this immersive journey, where the Tamsui River weaves tales of serenity and history. Join me as we uncover the timeless charm and cultural treasures of Tamsuis, creating memories that will linger in your heart forever.

A Riverside Oasis

Our day trip in Tamsuis begins with the gentle murmur of the Tamsui River, a soothing melody that sets the tone for a serene escape. As we stroll along the riverside promenade, the crisp air carries the scent of the water and the sight of boats gently gliding across the surface. The Tamsui River is not just a body of water; it is the lifeblood of the town, connecting history, culture, and nature in harmonious unity.

Fort San Domingo: A Window to the Past

Our first stop takes us to Fort San Domingo, an architectural gem that reflects Taiwan's colonial history. The vibrant red-bricked fortress stands tall against the backdrop of the azure sky, a testament to the region's strategic importance. As we explore the historical site, the remnants of the past come alive, painting a vivid picture of Taiwan's colonial era.

Strolling Tamsui Old Street

Next, we venture into the heart of Tamsuis, Tamsui Old Street. The narrow alleys are adorned with traditional tea houses, local eateries, and charming souvenir shops. The aroma of freshly brewed tea and the sizzle of street food tempt our senses, inviting us to indulge in local delicacies. Try the famous fish balls, oyster omelets, and pineapple cakes, each bite a burst of flavor that lingers on your taste buds.

Tranquil Moments at Tamsui Customs Wharf

Our journey leads us to Tamsui Customs Wharf, a haven of serenity and artistic inspiration. As we explore the area, colorful murals and street art captivate our gaze, infusing the riverside landscape with vibrant energy. The blend of old and new architecture adds to the unique ambiance, creating an ideal spot for photographers and art enthusiasts.

Sunset Magic on Lover's Bridge

As the day progresses, we find ourselves on Lover's Bridge, a must-visit spot to witness the breathtaking Tamsui sunset. The sky transforms into a canvas of vivid colors, casting a magical glow on the river and its surroundings. Couples and friends gather to share this enchanting moment, capturing the essence of love and togetherness.

Tamsui Fisherman's Wharf: Coastal Charms

For a touch of coastal beauty, we head to Tamsui Fisherman's Wharf, where wooden boardwalks lead us to charming lighthouses and bustling seafood markets. The picturesque views of the river and sea create a tranquil setting, allowing us to unwind and bask in the coastal charms of Tamsuis.

Embracing the Essence of Tamsuis

As our day trip comes to an end, we find ourselves reflecting on the timeless charm, cultural treasures, and tranquil moments that define Tamsuis. The town's beauty has left an indelible mark on our hearts, and the allure of its peaceful allure beckons us to return and explore more of its hidden wonders.

Tamsuis is a destination that embodies the harmony of history, nature, and culture. As an insider, I assure you that this day trip will awaken your senses, ignite your curiosity, and leave you with a profound appreciation for the hidden gems of this riverside oasis. So, come, immerse yourself in the tranquility, and let Tamsuis take you on an unforgettable journey of exploration and delight. Happy adventures!

Yangmingshan

Get ready for an extraordinary day of exploration and natural beauty as we embark on a thrilling day trip to Yangmingshan, a breathtaking national park just a stone's throw away from Taipei. As an insider, I am thrilled to be your guide on this immersive journey, where the lush landscapes and volcanic wonders of Yangmingshan unfold before your eyes. Join me as we uncover the hidden treasures and picturesque sights that make Yangmingshan a nature lover's paradise.

A Verdant Welcome

Our adventure begins as we ascend the winding roads that lead us to the heart of Yangmingshan. The air becomes crisp and refreshing, and the scenery transforms into a lush green wonderland. The dense foliage of tall bamboo and evergreen trees surround us, creating a sense of tranquility and seclusion.

Flowering Beauties: Yangmingshan Flower Clock

Our first stop takes us to the iconic Yangmingshan Flower Clock, where a stunning display of vibrant blooms greets us with their exquisite beauty. As the hands of the clock gently move, the flowers create a mesmerizing tapestry of colors, capturing the essence of Yangmingshan's floral wonders.

Qingtiangang: A Surreal Grassland

Next, we venture to Qingtiangang, a surreal grassland plateau that seems like a painting come to life. The gentle undulations of the grassy terrain extend as far as the eye can see, dotted with grazing cattle and the occasional grazing sheep. The view of the rolling hills against the backdrop of the distant mountains is a sight that leaves us in awe of Mother Nature's artistry.

A Symphony of Color: Lengshuikeng Hot Springs

As we continue our journey, we find ourselves at Lengshuikeng, a volcanic wonderland boasting a symphony of colors. The hot springs in varying hues of turquoise, emerald, and orange bubble up from the ground, creating a mesmerizing spectacle. The natural steam rising from the springs adds to the mystical ambiance, inviting us to soak in the healing properties of these mineral-rich waters.

Xiaoyoukeng: Witnessing Geothermal Wonders

Our adventure takes an adventurous turn as we head to Xiaoyoukeng, a geothermal area where fumaroles release puffs of sulfuric steam into the air. The earth's rumblings and the scent of sulfur create an otherworldly experience, transporting us to a realm of raw geological power. The wooden boardwalks provide safe passage as we witness nature's forces at work.

Refreshing Scents: Bamboo Lake

A serene oasis awaits us at Bamboo Lake, where the fragrant aroma of bamboo fills the air. The tranquil lake reflects the surrounding bamboo groves, creating a peaceful setting for quiet contemplation. We walk along the serene paths, the soft rustling of bamboo leaves providing a soothing soundtrack to our journey.

The Crown Jewel: Qixing Mountain

Our day trip culminates at Qixing Mountain, the crown jewel of Yangmingshan. As we hike to the peak, the panoramic views of Taipei city, the ocean, and the mountains take our breath away. Standing atop Qixing Mountain, we feel on top of the world, as if we can touch the sky and embrace the beauty that stretches far and wide.

Embracing Nature's Bounty

As we bid farewell to Yangmingshan, we carry with us the memories of lush landscapes, colorful hot springs, and the wonders of the volcano. The day spent in this nature's paradise has left an indelible mark, and the allure of Yangmingshan beckons us to return and explore more of its breathtaking treasures.

Yangmingshan is a haven of natural wonders, where the beauty of the earth's creations unfolds in all its glory. As an insider, I assure you that this day trip will awaken your senses, ignite your spirit of adventure, and leave you with a profound appreciation for the natural wonders of this captivating national park. So, come, immerse yourself in the beauty, and let Yangmingshan take you on an unforgettable journey of exploration and enchantment. Happy adventures!

Pingxi

Prepare for a day filled with enchantment and discovery as we embark on an immersive day trip to Pingxi, a quaint and picturesque destination nestled in the mountains of Taiwan. As an insider, I am thrilled to be your guide on this captivating journey, where the allure of old railway lines, majestic waterfalls, and sky lantern traditions will leave you spellbound. Join me as we unravel the hidden treasures and charming sights that make Pingxi a true gem worth exploring.

A Train Ride through Time

Our adventure commences as we hop on the Pingxi Railway Line, a historic train journey that traverses scenic landscapes and quaint villages. The rhythmic chug of the vintage locomotive sets the tone for a nostalgic voyage through time. As we pass through lush green forests and idyllic countryside, we can't help but feel a sense of wonder at the simple beauty of the journey.

Old-World Charm: Shifen Old Street

Our first stop is at Shifen Old Street, a delightful alleyway adorned with traditional red lanterns and quaint shop fronts. The charm of this historic street takes us back to a bygone era, where the aroma of local snacks fills the air. We indulge in mouthwatering treats like peanut candies, mochi, and ice cream rolls, savoring every flavor like a cherished memory.

Wishing Skyward: Sky Lanterns in Shifen

Next, we experience the mesmerizing tradition of releasing sky lanterns into the sky. As we pen our wishes and dreams on colorful lanterns, a sense of hope and unity fills the air. Together, we release our lanterns, watching them soar higher and higher until they become tiny specks in the vast sky. It's a moment that stays with us, reminding us of the power of dreams and aspirations.

A Glimpse of History: Jingan Suspension Bridge

Our journey takes an adventurous turn as we venture to the Jingan Suspension Bridge, a historic landmark swaying gently over a lush gorge. The wooden planks creak beneath our feet, reminding us of the countless travelers who have crossed this bridge over the years. As we gaze down at the tranquil river below, we feel a sense of connection to the past and the natural wonders that surround us.

Cascading Beauty: Shifen Waterfall

A breathtaking sight awaits us at Shifen Waterfall, Taiwan's most famous waterfall. The cascading waters plunge dramatically into the pool below, creating a mesmerizing spectacle of nature's power. We feel the cool mist on our skin as we stand in awe of this majestic wonder, capturing the moment in our hearts and cameras.

Quietude in Pingxi Old Street

As we return to Pingxi, we find ourselves in Pingxi Old Street, a charming haven that exudes tranquility and a sense of community. The quiet streets and traditional shops invite us to explore and take in the essence of local life. We find hidden gems in the form of handicrafts, artworks, and delectable snacks that tempt us to indulge in more local flavors.

Lingering at Lingjiao Waterfall

Our final stop takes us to Lingjiao Waterfall, a lesser-known gem that rewards us with its natural beauty. As we trek through lush greenery, the sound of rushing water guides us to this serene oasis. The cascading waterfall creates a soothing ambiance, offering a perfect spot for quiet reflection and rejuvenation.

Embracing the Enchantment of Pingxi

As our day trip to Pingxi comes to an end, we carry with us the memories of old-world charm, cascading waterfalls, and the magic of sky lanterns. The allure of Pingxi beckons us to return, promising more hidden treasures and moments of enchantment.

Pingxi is a destination where nature and tradition intertwine, leaving an indelible mark on our hearts. As an insider, I assure you that this day trip will awaken your senses, ignite your sense of adventure, and leave you with a profound appreciation for the enchanting wonders of this picturesque mountain town. So, come, immerse yourself in the charm, and let Pingxi take you on an unforgettable journey of exploration and delight. Happy adventures!

Practical Tips and Know-How

Navigating Taipei's Efficient Transportation

Welcome to Taipei, a bustling metropolis where the heartbeat of the city resonates through its efficient transportation network. As an insider, I am thrilled to be your guide on this journey, where you'll experience the seamless blend of modernity and tradition that Taipei's transportation system offers. Join me as we navigate the city's efficient transportation and discover how getting around Taipei is an adventure in itself.

The MRT: A Symphony of Speed

Our journey begins with the Taipei Metro (MRT), an intricate web of train lines that connect every corner of the city. As we step onto the platform, the rhythmic chime signals the train's arrival. The MRT is like a symphony of speed and precision, whisking passengers from one destination to another with impressive efficiency. The sleek trains zip through the underground tunnels, seamlessly transporting us from the bustling heart of the city to the tranquil outskirts.

Ubiquitous YouBike Stations

Venturing above ground, we encounter the iconic YouBike stations scattered throughout Taipei. These vibrant orange bicycles are a beloved mode of transportation for locals and visitors alike. With a simple tap on the touchscreen, we unlock the bike and pedal through the city streets, feeling the wind in our hair as we pass by historical landmarks and modern skyscrapers. YouBike offers a unique perspective of Taipei's urban landscape, allowing us to immerse ourselves in the vibrant street life.

A Symphony of Bus Routes

As we explore further, we discover the extensive bus network that complements the MRT system. The colorful buses weave through the city's arteries, providing an affordable and convenient way to reach destinations beyond the reach of the MRT. We hop on a bus and find ourselves on a journey of discovery, passing through charming neighborhoods, local markets, and verdant parks.

The Elegance of the Maokong Gondola

For a taste of elegance, we board the Maokong Gondola, an aerial cable car that takes us to the picturesque tea-growing hills of Maokong. As we ascend, the cityscape below transforms into a panoramic vista of rolling hills and lush tea plantations. The gentle swaying of the gondola adds to the tranquil experience, and we savor every moment of this scenic escape.

The Spirit of the Traditional Zhongshan Line

Our journey wouldn't be complete without a ride on the Zhongshan Line, a historic train that preserves the spirit of Taipei's traditional past. As we board this vintage train, the wooden seats and classic design transport us to a bygone era. The train rattles along the tracks, taking us on a charming ride that pays homage to Taipei's heritage.

River Cruises: The Waterways of Taipei

To experience Taipei from a different perspective, we embark on a river cruise along the Tamsui River. The tranquil waterways offer a unique view of the city's skyline, adorned with a harmonious blend of modern architecture and ancient temples. The gentle lapping of the water and the cool breeze create a serene atmosphere, making the river cruise a moment of relaxation amidst the bustling cityscape.

The Magic of Taipei's Night Markets

As the sun sets, Taipei's transportation network continues to facilitate our adventures. We hop on the MRT or a bus and head to one of Taipei's famous night markets. The energy and vibrancy of the night markets are palpable, and the scent of street food tantalizes our taste buds. Navigating through the bustling alleys, we sample local delicacies, shop for souvenirs, and soak in the lively atmosphere.

Embracing Taipei's Efficient Harmony

As our journey through Taipei's efficient transportation comes to an end, we realize that getting around the city is an adventure filled with convenience and excitement. Taipei's transportation system seamlessly weaves together tradition and modernity, offering an experience that is as dynamic as the city itself.

Taipei's efficient transportation network is a testament to the city's commitment to seamless travel for its residents and visitors. As an insider, I assure you that navigating Taipei is an opportunity to embrace the rhythm of the city and discover its many facets. So, come, hop on the MRT, pedal a YouBike, and glide on a gondola as you let Taipei's efficient harmony guide you through an unforgettable journey of exploration and delight. Happy travels!

Finding the Perfect Accommodation

Affordable Accommodations:

In Taipei, consider staying in hostels or budget hotels located in popular neighborhoods like Ximending or Daan. These areas offer easy access to public transportation and a vibrant atmosphere. Look for guesthouses or Airbnb rentals in local neighborhoods for a more authentic experience at a lower cost. Booking accommodations in advance can often lead to better deals.

Savvy Dining Choices:

Taipei is a food lover's paradise, and you can enjoy delicious meals without overspending. Opt for local eateries, night markets, and food stalls where you can try an array of mouthwatering dishes at budget-friendly prices. Popular night markets like Shilin and Raohe offer a variety of affordable and delectable street food options.

Utilize Public Transportation:

Taipei's public transportation system is efficient and cost-effective. Purchase an EasyCard, a reloadable transportation card that offers discounts on MRT (subway) fares, buses, and even some convenience stores. It's a convenient way to get around the city without breaking the bank.

Free and Low-Cost Attractions:

Take advantage of Taipei's many free and low-cost attractions. Visit iconic landmarks like Taipei 101 and Chiang Kai-shek Memorial Hall, which offer stunning views and photo opportunities without an entry fee. Explore traditional temples such as Longshan Temple and Bao'an Temple to immerse yourself in local culture.

Embrace Nature's Beauty:

Enjoy the natural beauty surrounding Taipei without spending much. Hike up Elephant Mountain (Xiangshan) for a breathtaking view of the city skyline, especially during sunset. Visit Yangmingshan National Park for serene hot springs, hiking trails, and picturesque scenery.

Museum and Gallery Hopping:

Many museums and galleries in Taipei offer free entry or have discounted admission on certain days. The National Palace Museum and Taipei Fine Arts Museum are worth exploring for art and history enthusiasts on a budget.

Affordable Souvenir Shopping:

For budget-friendly souvenirs, visit local markets like Shilin Night Market or the underground shopping streets at Taipei Main Station. These places offer a wide range of affordable trinkets, clothing, and unique Taiwanese gifts to take home.

Discount Passes and Tourist Cards:

Consider purchasing Taipei Fun Pass or Taipei Unlimited Fun Pass, which offer unlimited rides on public transportation and free or discounted access to popular attractions. These passes can help you save money and streamline your sightseeing.

Be Mindful of Budget:

Keep track of your spending and set a daily budget to avoid overspending. With many tempting options in Taipei, it's easy to get carried away, but being mindful of your budget ensures you stay on track.

Explore Local Markets and Parks:

Get a glimpse of daily life in Taipei by exploring local markets like Ningxia Night Market or Dongmen Market. These markets offer a variety of local produce, snacks, and affordable meals. Taipei's parks, such as Da'an Forest Park, are perfect for leisurely strolls and picnics.

By following these insider tips, you can experience the best of Taipei while staying within your budget. Embrace the city's culture, cuisine, and attractions without worrying about overspending, making your Taipei adventure an unforgettable and affordable experience. Happy travels!

Mandarin Phrases for Everyday Conversations

Mastering Basic Greetings:

As an insider in Taipei, mastering basic greetings is key to starting conversations on the right foot. Begin with "Nǐ hǎo" (你好) for a simple "hello." Add "Zàijiàn" (再见) for "goodbye" to leave a lasting impression of courtesy and respect.

Polite Phrases and Expressions:

Politeness is highly regarded in Taiwanese culture. Include "Xièxiè" (谢谢) for "thank you" and "Bù kèqì" (不客气) for "you're welcome" in your conversational repertoire. Demonstrating gratitude and graciousness will endear you to the locals.

Asking for Directions:

Navigating the bustling streets of Taipei can be an adventure in itself. Learn "Qǐng wèn, ...zěnme zǒu?" (请问，...怎么走?) to politely ask for directions. Fill in the blank with your destination, and locals will be happy to assist you on your way.

Ordering Food with Confidence:

Eating in Taipei is a delightful experience, but ordering in Mandarin can be intimidating. Master "Wǒ yào yīgè ..." (我要一个...) to confidently order one of your favorite dishes. Replace the ellipsis with the name of the dish you desire, and you'll be savoring the city's culinary delights in no time.

Asking for the Price:

In Taipei's vibrant markets, haggling is common, and knowing how to ask for the price is essential. Learn "Duōshǎo qián?" (多少钱?) to inquire about the cost of items. Polite bargaining can lead to fantastic deals and a fun cultural exchange with the vendors.

Expressing Gratitude for Recommendations:

When locals recommend their favorite places, show your appreciation with "Tīng nǐ de, hǎo zhǔyì!" (听你的，好主意!) which means "Thanks for the suggestion, good idea!" Locals will be pleased to see you embrace their recommendations.

Introducing Yourself:

Making new friends is an enriching part of travel. Introduce yourself with "Wǒ jiào ..." (我叫...) followed by your name. This simple phrase opens the door to meaningful connections with locals.

Excusing Yourself Politely:

Sometimes, you might need to excuse yourself in social situations. Learn "Bù hǎo yìsi" (不好意思) for "excuse me" or "I'm sorry" to maintain politeness and respect during your interactions.

Expressing Enjoyment:

After a delicious meal or a wonderful experience, show your delight with "Hěn hǎochī!" (很好吃!) for "it's delicious" or "Hěn yǒuyìsi!" (很有意思!) for "it's interesting." Locals will appreciate your enthusiasm for their culture.

Parting Words:

As you bid farewell to newfound friends, use "Zàijiàn, wǒ zǒu le" (再见，我走了) to say "Goodbye, I'm leaving." It's a thoughtful way to express your gratitude and leave with fond memories of your encounters in Taipei.

By embracing these Mandarin phrases for everyday conversations, you'll not only enhance your travel experiences in Taipei but also foster meaningful connections with the locals. Speaking their language, even in simple terms, shows your respect and appreciation for their culture. Enjoy your time in Taipei, and may these insider tips lead you to delightful and heartwarming exchanges throughout your journey. Safe travels!

Conclusion

As we conclude this journey through the vibrant cityscape of Taipei in 2024, we are filled with a sense of awe and wonder at the enchanting experiences that await every traveler in this lively urban hub. In this ultimate Taipei Travel Guide, we have delved into the heart of the city, uncovering its hidden gems, rich traditions, and modern marvels.

From the bustling night markets that tempt our taste buds with delectable delights to the tranquil temples that offer moments of serenity and reflection, Taipei has captured our hearts in its unique blend of old and new. We have embraced the warmth of the locals' greetings, felt the camaraderie of shared laughter, and immersed ourselves in the beauty of local customs and etiquette.

As the city evolves with each passing year, we know that Taipei in 2024 holds infinite possibilities for even more exciting discoveries and unforgettable adventures. From the soaring heights of Taipei 101 to the lush greenery of Yangmingshan, every step taken in Taipei is a step towards embracing its dynamic spirit and cultural diversity.

May this guide serve as your compass and companion as you venture forth into the bustling streets and captivating neighborhoods of Taipei. Whether you are a first-time visitor or a returning traveler, let this guide be your key to unlocking the heart and soul of this remarkable city.

As we bid farewell to Taipei in 2024, we carry with us the memories of the mesmerizing skyline, the tantalizing aromas of street food, and the genuine smiles of the locals who made us feel at home. Let us hold these cherished moments close to our hearts, and may they inspire us to continue exploring, connecting, and embracing the world with open arms and a spirit of curiosity.

So, dear travelers, until we meet again for the next adventure, let Taipei's energy and warmth linger in your memories, ready to ignite your wanderlust whenever it calls. Happy travels, and may Taipei always hold a special place in your heart as a city that invites you to discover the extraordinary in the everyday!

Made in the USA
Coppell, TX
30 April 2024

31869993R00089